STAGE FIGHT

FOR TEACHERS

How to Punch Your Fears
of Public Speaking in the Face!

Cody Smith
AND **Shasta Smith**

Stage Fight For Teachers: How to Punch Your Fears of Public Speaking In the Face!
/ By Cody Smith and Shasta Smith

Paperback Edition ISBN-13: 978-0-9996942-7-5

Ebook Edition ISBN-13: 978-0-9996942-8-2

Library of Congress Control Number is on file with the publisher.

Published by Nelaco Press

Printed in the United States of America

Book design by Layne Smith Design

The stories and experiences captured in this book have been recreated from memory some of which were abridged to better communicate what was said or what transpired.

DEDICATION

To those with the unique gift to touch the minds and hearts of students everywhere.

Thank you.

- Cody

To my sister, Dusti. You are the most selfless person I know. Thank you for always believing in me. I am honored to be your little sister. I love you forever.

- Shasta

Table Of Contents

INTRODUCTION

Public speaking is scary. Period. There aren't many venues out there requiring you to be completely vulnerable. Every mistake you make is public knowledge, recorded in the minds of your audience. Every fumble, mumble, and stutter could bring judgement.

If we make a mistake on stage, the impact is far greater than making a mistake from the comfort of our couch, in our classroom, or around close friends and family. In front of a crowd, we amplify the consequences of completely sucking at something as simple as speaking.

Thus, we build mental barriers to filter out any reason or opportunity to develop public speaking skills. We view those opportunities as threats to our lifestyle, to our comfort, to our current status quo. We avoid these opportunities at all costs.

When the PTA president cancels the meeting you were asked to speak at or when someone else volunteers to speak at the teacher cadet forum before a random name is drawn, we react as if a jury deemed us "not guilty." A sigh of relief fills every crevice of our being, ending with an even bigger exhale while saying, "Oh, thank God." The sun shines once again, and we can go back to the way things were. The way things "should" be within our own sphere of comfort.

If you're sick and tired of feeling like you just can't get a grip on yourself in front of an audience, or you wish the days leading up to a speaking engagement weren't filled with dread and fear, then let this book guide you to change that.

Maybe your past experiences with public speaking could be summed up in two words: stage fright. I want you to know I've been there. I struggled for years to speak confidently front and center.

It all started with a terrible performance in middle school. I carried that memory with me and re-lived it every time I had to speak to a crowd thereafter.

Every second on a stage of any kind felt like suffering. I dreaded staring into the eyes of my audience, and I couldn't understand why it was so hard for me. I was literally afraid to say words— words! I responded as if someone were holding a gun to my head.

Now I can address a crowd confidently. However, I want to be very transparent with you: I am not a professional speaker. I don't have 20 years' experience as a public speaker. I've never been paid to speak. Nor have I ever given a keynote speech. While I hope to have these experiences one day, I can't list them on my current resume.

What I can say is that following the steps and exercises laid out in this book changed me and they can change you, too.

Before, I was someone who would rather be the guy in the casket versus the poor soul who had to give the eulogy.

Following what's in the chapters to come helped me become someone who could pitch a business idea in college and raise over $17k to turn that idea into reality.

Without overcoming my fears of public speaking, I would never have been able to do that. Overcoming my fears also raised my confidence through the roof. I don't dread having to speak anymore. I look forward to speaking. I want that same result for you.

I want you to walk out on stage standing tall and confident. I want to see you conquer your fears of public speaking.

I promise you here and now if you read and implement the steps found in this book, you WILL become a courageous speaker—in fact, it's impossible to not become one after you do so.

To start, you must decide whether you want to become a confident, courageous speaker by reading this book, or if you want to continue in fear and cast this book aside. You get to choose whether your life will be one big stage fright or whether you will own it, making it your very own stage fight.

Get ready to conquer your fears of public speaking by taking action today and choosing to read this book to become a confident, courageous speaker.

Welcome to the Stage Fight Club where we punch our fears IN. THE. FACE. Read on.

SECTION 1

—

SHASTA'S STORY

CHAPTER 1

A UNIQUE VOICE

I have always considered myself an enthusiastic person. Maybe it's my inner cheerleader, but I am usually overly excited about things no one else cares about. This can make social situations a bit awkward. Additionally, I am a perfectionist in every sense of the word. So in a conversation, I become overly excited and inwardly terrified that secretly I am the person at the party everyone avoids talking to.

Growing up, I hid my insecurities in the shadow of my amazing older brother, Ky. If my brother had a superpower, it would be his ability to make everyone in a room love him or secretly want to be him. Even though I was awkward, everyone kind of let it slide because I was his little sister and that made me "cool" by association. However, when I went to college, I vowed to finally step out of the shadows and "find myself".

So, the only logical first step of self-discovery for an enthusiastic perfectionist like myself would be to meet new people and conquer one of their deepest, darkest fears—public speaking.

Now I know that public speaking is one of the top fears for most people, but let me preface by saying: not only am I socially awkward with a deep-seeded fear of being perceived as incompetent or stupid, but the actual sound of my voice is politely referred to as "unique". Think Tammy II from *Parks and Recreation* unique. Basically, unique is the polite Southern way of saying my voice is annoyingly high pitched.

Therefore, you can see how my overly enthusiastic personality, my inner perfectionist, and my unique voice made me one to shy away from public speaking. But seeing as how speech class is a requirement for graduation, I decided that I would take the Art of Public Speaking my very first semester.

I also decided to take this class at eight in the morning, hindsight being what it is: if you are an overly enthusiastic person, DO NOT take a speech class at 8am because you will be one of the very few people excited to be there, AND EVERYONE ELSE WILL HATE YOU!

Our first assignment was to prepare a 3-5 minute presentation about ourselves. Simple enough. However, my perfectionist life motto is if you fail to prepare, you prepare to fail. So, I prepared about 80 notecards which were all color-coded, numbered, and organized, as well as a presentation board outlining all of my key points.

I was prepared and therefore ready to ace this assignment.

I would captivate my audience with a joke, put the room at ease, and transition seamlessly through my key points, and conclude with a quote.

But ya know what they say about the best laid plans...

I arrived early the day of my speech to run over my outline once more and decided that I would volunteer first so my nerves wouldn't get the best of me. I gripped my notes tightly, smiled just like I practiced, and began with my opening joke.

Ten words. Ten words was all it took for me to crumble.

I told my opening joke and the room fell silent. No one laughed. Not even my professor. It's safe to say in that awkward silence, instead of captivating my audience, I held them captive in a series of unfortunate events. At this point my fight or flight response took over, and I began to fumble, talking faster and faster, rambling on about my cows. I got midway through my speech when my fight response transformed into enthusiastic energy. One thing you should know about enthusiastic people is we tend to talk with our hands. As I am motioning with my hands, I begin to drop Every. Single. Notecard.

People like me need notecards! I am not a fly-by-the seat of your pants kind of gal.

At this point, I am completely mortified. I am sweating. I feel like I can no longer breathe or form coherent sentences. My inner perfectionist is screaming: You look like an IDIOT! ABORT! ABORT! I could no longer stay and fight. I had to fly to anywhere besides the front of that room.

The thing about college is that people are less likely to make you feel better. There is no participation trophy, no cookie, no gold star. It's not like in elementary school where people tell you "good job" even though you sucked. And, I sucked hard that day. I sat back down in my seat trying not to breakdown in tears as I listened to my classmates stroll up to the podium and dazzle us with their quick wit and sparkling personality.

I was ashamed. I was embarrassed.

Worst of all, I was a failure.

—Shasta's Note—

This was the MOST EMBARRASSING MOMENT of my life (you're welcome).

CHAPTER 2

WHEN A WOMAN CHANGES HER HAIR

I would like to say that after this traumatic, humiliating event, I took my epic failure in stride and used it as a learning experience. And perhaps, with some retrospect, I now see it was a defining moment in my life.

However, all I did that night was eat my weight in Ben and Jerry's Chocolate Chip Cookie Dough ice cream and drink enough boxed red wine to make me think I could dance like Beyoncé. However, while belting out some old-school TLC, I had a moment of clarity, and did the only logical thing I could think to do—I scheduled a hair appointment. Because everyone knows when a woman changes her hair, she's about to conquer the world.

However, I didn't want to conquer just any world; I wanted to conquer the teaching world. And for all of you non-teachers reading this book, stop reading this and go thank a teacher.

I'll wait...

Now that we've all thanked our past teachers, this is the part in the book where I become very transparent with you.

The teaching world is HARD. Tough days make you want to curl up under your desk and scream, "This job is too much!" As I am typing, I can think of so many reasons I shouldn't write this book on behalf of teachers. Who am I to write a book? Who am I to tell my story? DO I EVEN WANT TO TELL MY STORY? I am a literal SPEECH HORROR STORY!

But, my courage to do so comes from my belief that our profession desperately needs to rise up and fight. And although being the voice of that fight is terrifying, I hope telling my teacher story is an invitation for others in my profession to do the same because only with collective efficacy can we truly see the change in education that both ourselves and our students deserve. So, if you're ready to do more than just #wearREDforEd, if you're ready to stand up and fight then Welcome to Stage Fight: Teacher's Edition where we have crafted the perfect lesson plan on how to punch our public speaking fears IN. THE. FACE. Read On!

—Shasta's Note—

If you're ever in need of a pick-me-up, Ben and Jerry's Chocolate Chip Cookie Dough is cheap and amazing.

CHAPTER 3

GRAVITATIONAL MADNESS

One of my favorite movies of all time is The Dark Knight. Yes, I was in love with Heath Ledger's performance (well secretly, I loved him since *10 Things I Hate About You*), but one of the most captivating moments in *The Dark Knight* was it's opening sequence. I know, I know, the ending was spectacular, but be honest: did you predict the school bus scene? (I didn't think so). I left the theater inspired by the film's opening because the first five minutes hooked me, and the next sequence of events set the tone for what the Joker refers to as "gravitational madness".

The Joker explains that madness is like gravity it only takes a little push for people to either become consumed by their fears or overcome their fears. Lightbulb moment: to conquer the teaching world, I only needed a little gravitational push to overcome my public speaking fears. (Cue my inner cheerleader. Shasta, what's your battle cry? V-I-C-T-O-R-Y!)

—Shasta's Note—

Heath Ledger is the best Joker hands down!

CHAPTER 4

YOUTUBE CHANGED MY LIFE

Now remember, I am a perfectionist. So, my little gravitational push had to be more like a shove if I was ever going to try public speaking again. After reading every teaching book that made the New York Times best seller list that year and watching Rita Pierson's TED Talk Video and Todd Whittaker's YouTube Video on repeat, my gravitational push would come from an unlikely source.

My life was forever changed by a YouTube video that spoke about "finding your why." Once we find our "why", it will quiet the voices of self-doubt in our head that tells us we are not good enough. Most importantly, he spoke on the importance of telling others your "why".

The speaker said, "If we won't stand up and speak about our 'why', others will never advocate for our 'why'."

My "why" comes from my deep seeded belief that education can change the world. Not many other professions get to leave a mark on something much greater than themselves and their community.

This “why” made me “mad” enough to believe that the girl with the annoyingly high-pitched voice could not only speak but advocate for her educational beliefs.

I don’t want you to think that I watched a YouTube video and then BAM—pulled a Beyoncé and transformed from a socially awkward person to Sasha Fierce—a courageous, amazing public speaker. I am still slightly terrified every time I step onto a stage. However, my “why” out cheers my perfectionist head voice.

It whispers to me, “You don’t have to be perfect. You just have to be passionate.”

So instead of being consumed by my fears, I become encouraged by my passions.

I began telling my “why” to anyone that would listen. I spoke at my school faculty meetings, PTA events, district professional development workshops, college campuses, local community events, and educational conferences.

With each presentation, I carved my own path, my own voice, my own platform. And hopefully, I will share my platform on the biggest stage of all as South Carolina’s State Teacher of the Year.

As excited as I am about advocating for education and sharing my “why”, I am and will always be a teacher first, not a public speaker. That’s why I’ve teamed up to co-teach this lesson with Cody so he can teach you everything you need to know about the art of public speaking.

So, if you are ready to create your own teaching platform, to share your “why”, to punch your fears of public speaking in the face, READ ON!

SECTION 2

—

UNDERSTANDING AND CHANGING YOUR PERSPECTIVE OF FEAR

CHAPTER 5

MY MISSION

As Shasta just said, she's the teacher and I'm the public speaker. But it certainly has not always been that way...

It started with a hard-to-forget first public speaking experience in middle school that scarred me for years, and it led up to college where I finally took some drastic measures to forever punch my fears of public speaking in the face. This is a story I dive deeper into in the original *Stage Fight* book.

However, this book isn't about me. This book is about Shasta and teachers just like her who struggled with their fears of speaking in front of a crowd. Teachers who have something to say and want a platform to speak on to better the world of education for the next generation.

I believe anyone with a heart to teach has an innate drive to share and expand the knowledge and understanding of others. It's somethings that seems wired inside their DNA. A drive to discover what it takes to open doors to allow someone to learn.

As culture and technology changes, so does the tactics and strategies to teach the young minds in our societies. Once shared, these new tactics and strategies may go on to hopefully become some of the best practices that can benefit everyone. But only if they are shared.

Those most likely to uncover these new approaches to teaching are those who teach day in and day out. However, often a nagging force appears preventing those with something worth sharing from speaking up. I refer to that force as our inner coward-self. The part of us that feeds on fears and doubt. That inner voice that likes to take jabs and a mean right hook into our blind spot. It strikes the face of our confidence and self-worth, especially when we try to stand tall in front of an audience to speak. An audience that needs to hear what we have to say and share.

We've all got a coward-self. A part of us that stops us from doing what we want to do. For a lot of us, myself and Shasta included, we've let our coward-self take the lead when it came time to face our fears of public speaking.

Luckily it doesn't have to be that way. You can become a courageous speaker and it's my goal and mission to help get you there. I'll walk you through exactly what you need to do to get over your fears in the shortest amount of time as possible.

Let's face it, if there's anything teachers don't have a lot of is extra time. We expect a lot from our teachers and the last thing they need is more on their plate of things to do.

I've laid out the Stage Fight Method to accommodate even the busiest of people, so they too can fit public speaking fear punching into their schedules without an incredible amount of strain on their time.

Before I hand you back over to Shasta for some not so obvious teacher's tips, I'm going to walk you through how you can punch your fears of public speaking in the face. Keep in mind I refer to my experience dealing with my fear of public speaking in the upcoming chapters.

Up first, we'll go over the mindset needed for public speaking before getting into the how-to. Consider this the warm up before the big fight.

Get ready because your first opponent is your fear.

CHAPTER 6

WHAT IS FEAR?

Let's start by describing the feeling of fear for what it really is: a bodily response to a perceived threat or consequence—whether real or not.

In fact, we don't even have to identify the specific fear for our body to react. We just perceive a threat, and our body reacts.

There are different levels in response to fear. Anywhere from butterflies in your stomach to a full-blown anxiety attack. Two people might step out onto the same stage, facing the same audience, with the same message, with the same level of knowledge of that message, but the two could respond completely differently.

One speaker might talk confidently, connect with the audience, and appear quite comfortable. The other speaker, however, might be stricken with fear, mutter and stumble through their speech, and appear very uncomfortable on stage.

Did the threat change? Nope! The threat of possible failure, of the audience not reacting, was constant for both speakers. The difference was in their individual perception of the threat.

The confident speaker most likely focused on delivering a message that would benefit his audience. He walked out on that stage, appreciative of his audience coming to hear him speak, and focused on his opportunity to inspire, persuade, or entertain the crowd. To him, speaking is an honor, and he looked forward to the moment he would speak his first word to his audience.

The other speaker did not approach the opportunity the same way. He did not really see it as an opportunity but more as a threat to his level of comfort and peace of mind. Every passing moment before he actually had to speak, the lump in his throat grew, making it impossible to swallow. Fearing every mistake he might make in front of his audience, he tried not to think about it. But the more he tried not to, the more he anticipated potential blunders, obsessing over it.

Every negative thought just kept adding to his already growing nerves and his reaction to his fears. By the time he was actually on stage, his perception became his reality as he started making the mistakes and blunders he couldn't stop thinking about.

The real lesson here is we chose how to perceive and react to the threat.

This is like the White Bear Phenomenon. The idea is simple. Picture a white bear in your head for five seconds. Now, for the next 60 seconds, DO NOT think about the white bear. Ready? Go!

60 seconds later

Okay, how did you do? Did you successfully not think about the white bear during the 60 seconds? If you are like most people, you probably had a hard time not thinking about the bear.

The more effort you put into not thinking about the white bear, the more you actually end up thinking about the white bear, getting to the point of obsessing about the bear.

Thus, focusing on the mistakes you don't want to make on stage makes it more likely you will mess up. So instead focus on being a courageous speaker who's excited and looking forward to speak and guess what might just happen. ☺

While you can choose not to focus on your fear, you should know your fears never go away. So don't think that if you don't focus on them, they will magically go away. The truth is. . .

CHAPTER 7

FEARS NEVER GO AWAY

Fears never truly go away. They are with us forever in a never-ending dance between us and what we fear most. Before I realized this on my own, I wanted a magic pill that would wipe my fears clean, leaving nothing behind.

That magic pill doesn't exist. However, I realized I could choose who takes the lead: fear or myself. There is never a choice to not dance with fear. That is unavoidable.

You, however, get to decide who gains control.

Let that sink in. No one else but you has everything you need to control your fear. It is a tango between you and your coward-self.

For years I had let my fears take the lead, and I was simply following their direction without question. But unfortunately, accepting that I had a choice did not make it easy to try to take the lead. I had been a follower for so long that taking the lead felt very uncomfortable.

Just like in all areas of life, you're going to make mistakes in taking charge. Don't expect to not step on your own toes the first go around. You may attempt and fail, falling back into letting your old self take the lead. Don't let that discourage you. Your power to choose is yours to keep forever. Even if you are failing consistently, one of your ultimate goals here is to start seeing failure in a whole new light. Maybe you'll even start to see failing as a positive experience.

CHAPTER 8

FAILING IS A BLESSING

So far we've worked to drive home the idea (or rather the fact) that we have a choice to make with how we view the world around us. We have a choice as to whether or not we will let fear call the shots. We get to choose and with that choice comes taking responsibility for our lives.

You get to choose how you see your failures. You can choose to see failure as something to avoid at all costs, to regret, to be embarrassed about—or you can choose to see it as a blessing, though that might be contrary to popular belief.

All throughout school, we are taught that failure is bad. The inability to test well in school could result in failing the grade altogether, requiring one to repeat that grade while all their friends and previous classmates move on to the next grade. Getting an "F" on a report card for failing several assignments and/or tests can cause one to feel inferior.

This problem can then escalate to future failing grades, leading to one not receiving scholarships and/or being rejected by several colleges, resulting in living a mediocre life working at a gas station, struggling with money, and constantly wishing and dreaming for better things.

This, of course, is an extreme exaggeration. Obviously good grades or bad grades do not control our fate, our success, or our happiness after graduation.

Rather than this ingrained idea that failure is a terrible thing, I want us to view failure from a different lens. Let's look at it as a part of life. A part of simply being alive. Not something to avoid but to expect. Life happens. Failure happens. To each and every one of us.

Can you think of one person who has never failed at something? Someone who is perfect and gets everything right the first time? If you have, I would love to meet your imaginary friend!

For now, I'm going to believe you have not met this perfect person. Everyone fails. Once you start to accept failure as a normal part of life, failing doesn't quite have the sting it once had.

Humans fail from the moment they are born. Just watch any infant learn to hold their head up right. At first it's a real struggle to balance that proportionally massive head on that spaghetti thin neck. Slowly but surely, they will gain more control and will no longer need assistance. Soon they can hold themselves upright while on their stomachs which becomes the prerequisite for crawling. A few more months, they master standing after much trial and error. Finally, they take that first step succeeded by yet another step reinforced by praise and excitement from two very proud parents.

The amount of "failures" leading up to that first step is staggering. Their failures even worth counting due to the sheer frequency of making mistake after mistake. Over and over that infant would try, fail, and try again, gaining valuable experience with each attempt.

Failure is not a means to an end but really a means to success. Failure from the beginning of all humans' lives is simply a way of life, and just a possible result of an attempt. That's it!

Adults are reluctant to try again after one failed attempt. Infants don't even question the result. They almost immediately try again without hesitation. I challenge you to see failure the same way—a step toward whatever your goal may be.

Start seeing failure as a blessing. A blessing that brings you closer to what you want. When viewed this way, failures take on a positive connotation. You're not likely to try and avoid a blessing. Why would you?

Once you change your belief of failure from negative to positive, failure becomes one less reason to not try something and one less reason to be afraid. That's one less reason why you should be punching your fears IN. THE. FACE.

You: If failing should be a positive thing, then why am I so afraid?

Now that's a great question, and the next chapter is going to answer that very question. Let's do this!

CHAPTER 9

WHY ARE YOU AFRAID?

Have you ever been around a four-year-old or five-year-old kid who has discovered that magical, one-word question to help quench their unquenchable curiosity: "why?"

This one word alone has the power to drive parents and loved ones alike absolutely insane if used correctly. Young children use that one question to help them understand and make sense of the world around them. We will use that very same question to help make sense of our fears.

This exercise can be done with anything you're afraid of. But for the purpose of this book, I want you to focus on your fear of public speaking.

Ask yourself why you are afraid, and then once you write down the answer, ask yourself why again.

This can be done with a partner asking you why after every answer or you can do it by yourself. I have my responses to the questions as an example.

Why am I afraid of public speaking?

- I'm afraid of looking stupid in front of a crowd and feeling judged.

Cool, why?

- Because looking stupid makes me feel uncomfortable.

Cool, why?

- Because feeling smart or at least appearing smart gives me a sense of worth.

Cool, why?

- Because having a sense of worth means to me that I have value and add value to others.

Cool, why?

- Because without a sense of value, I feel worthless.

Cool, why?

- If people think I'm worthless, no one will like me.

Cool, why?

- If no one likes me, then I might end up alone.

Ultimately, I'm afraid public speaking would reveal that I'm not as cool or important as I think I am. As if my sense of importance or worth was directly correlated to people liking me, and if people like me, then I have a good chance of having friends and not being alone.

Being on stage might reveal and expose all my flaws, and then no one would want to be around someone so imperfect. Sounds shallow, but that is something I desire: having value and thus being desired and accepted by others.

Once I recognized that, I actually felt better, to be honest. My fear was completely irrational, as most fears are. I'm not really afraid of speaking in public, I'm afraid of people realizing I'm not perfect. Everyone is flawed; no one is perfect, and we accept that of others, but sometimes we struggle to accept that of ourselves. My friends and family already know I'm not perfect, but accept me anyway.

Really take some time to get to the heart of your fears. It's important to do this before moving on to the next step where we walk through an exercise envisioning our worst fears coming to life.

BUT WHAT IF IT REALLY HAPPENS?

Now that we've discovered what our greatest fears are, we are going to imagine what would happen if our greatest fears morphed their way into reality. The most important thing you can do is have fun with this.

I want you to write out the worst thing that could happen if your greatest fears came to life. I provided an example from my life below.

Now what if I actually completely failed on stage (which I've already done several times before), but this time my failure was not something I nor my reputation could recover from. The result? All my friends decide from that point onward they never want to see me again, my family disowns me, and Uncle Sam decides to discharge me from the Air Force because there is no chance the military would want to associate the armed forces with a failure such as myself.

To top it off, all the major news channels around the world run a news bit on my catastrophic failure, globally destroying my reputation and self-worth complete with others shaming me on social media sites. I then receive what seems like an endless supply of death threats in the mail. Now that—that would be my worst fears coming to life.

The likelihood of that ever happening? Practically never which equals a 0.0000000002% chance of actually coming to life if I were to just do the rough math off the top of my head. I have better chances legally identifying myself as a shark than ever experiencing what I just described.

If I'm being honest, I actually had fun writing it down, and I recommend you do that same after going through the "why?" exercise getting to the root of your fears. There is a weird sense of liberation after getting it on paper, and the more ridiculous you can make your outcome the funner (not a word) it is.

Once you're done, share your worst fears coming to life with someone. It's almost guaranteed to result in sheer, joyful laughter for the both of you. Share it with a group if you dare. ☺

Laughing at your greatest fears turns them on their heads and helps you realize just how ridiculous they really are and how insane it is to let your fears stop you.

Do that exercise and get ready for the next part where we will write down what we would do if our greatest fears really happened. We're going to ask ourselves. . .

SO WHAT?

Once again, I encourage you to have fun with this. I definitely did, and so did my wife and my buddy, Robert, after I read it out loud to them. Below is my example of what I would do if my world came crashing down.

What would I seriously do if my worst fear became reality? First off, I would probably be homeless without a job to pay bills or friends or family to lean on for help. The first few nights would probably be awful trying to get restful sleep outside on a park bench somewhere.

On the bright side, I would have a lot more free time throughout my day to wander the city. I'd eventually get over my pride and search dumpsters for food, discovering a hoard of food thrown away by large-chain grocery stores because they simply reached their "sell by" date.

Food would no longer be an issue, and I believe I would share my haul of goods with my fellow homeless tribe members. I'd become a Robin Hood of sorts among the homeless. Finally, I'd grow out my beard, thus hiding my original identity as the global speaking failure.

Once I grew my confidence for taking care of myself and ridding myself of my attachment to money, I would roam the United States as a nomad finally quenching my never-ending thirst to travel and experience the world around me. I would take my time wherever I went truly taking in my surroundings rather than prior vacations with a set agenda rushing from place to place to get my "money's worth." My days would be full of actually living instead of living vicariously through work, emails, Facebook, and keeping up with the latest technology.

I would finally be able to live in the moment versus constantly worrying about the future or regretting what happened in the past. I wouldn't be addicted to constantly checking my phone for notifications or text messages. I would have genuine conversation with people, and I wouldn't care at all which way the economy was swinging. I would have no sense of the latest "news," which before just filled me with fear and depression.

Eventually, the world would forget about my blunder—as with all things. I would have an opportunity to rejoin society, but I believe I would rather continue on living as a nomad free of modern worries and obligation.

That doesn't seem so bad anymore. Going through that exercise put a smile on my face. It forced me to actually walk through my fears instead of filling my day with tasks to keep my mind off my biggest fears. What I thought was a 10 on a scale of worst possible outcomes quickly dwindled down well below a 3. Before I believed if I failed, my life would be over, but really my life would just take a different direction. I realized, even if that happened, I could dig myself out of that hole.

It changed my perspective, and I hope it helps change yours. Don't forget to share this exercise with someone. It's bound to get another laugh.

So far we've spent several chapters knee deep in our fears, understanding why they have prevented us from wanting to face them head on. In this next section of the book, we are going to get waist deep to talk about ways to drop kick our fears in the face. But first, I want you to know . . .

CHAPTER 10

NOT ALL FEARS ARE CREATED EQUAL

In the section discussing how to become a courageous speaker, I will challenge you to speak in public once a week in order to learn how to face your fears.

You: Well if facing my fears is the end goal, then can I just simply face a fear of mine once a week and skip this public speaking thing altogether?

Theoretically you could, but that is not bound to work out that well because not all fears are created equal. For example, the fear of asking someone out on a date via text message versus asking someone out in person versus asking someone out in front of all of her friends and yours have different levels and flavors of fear.

Asking someone out on a date over a text message leaves you feeling secure regardless of the outcome because you don't have to get rejected in person, and the feedback you get is limited to text, which means you don't get feedback from facial expression or tone of voice. (We'll ignore how asking someone out over text is totally not a groovy thing to do.)

Asking someone out in person has greater consequences if their answer is "no" because of the amount of feedback we receive from the pause in their response, the look in their eyes, the tone of their voice, their emotional response, and so on.

Compare that to asking them out in front of other people, which raises the stakes thereby raising the sting from a rejection since you're getting rejected in front of a crowd. Not only do you receive a feeling of rejection from the "rejecter" (you being the rejectee—yes, I just made up that word) but also from the response of those around you, which could exponentially make the rejection feel worse.

Given a choice, we would probably choose the level of fear by weighing out the risk of each situation, disregarding which environment might increase your odds of acceptance. Since we are more likely to avoid pain rather than chase pleasure, the text message option remains the "safest" choice.

We'll do the same thing every week when choosing which fear to face. The path of least resistance, the lowest level of fear, will almost always be the one we choose to tackle nine times out of ten. We'll lean toward gathering low-hanging fruit compared to slaying our greatest demons.

Public speaking is arguably one of the greatest demons we can slay because we are exposed and vulnerable. This makes public speaking one of the best choices to face your fears on a weekly basis. Even if it's not your greatest fear, it's bound to be high on your list; otherwise, you probably wouldn't be reading this book.

Facing your fears of public speaking on a weekly basis creates an incredible environment for you to land an uppercut while becoming a courageous speaker. Once conquered, lesser fears seem less significant and easier to face. Fears on par with public speaking don't seem as insurmountable.

Once you conquer public speaking, other fears show their true colors as merely mental obstacles you can overcome because you already know how.

SECTION 3

—

HOW TO FACE ANY FEAR

CHAPTER 11

GIVE YOURSELF PERMISSION TO SUCK

While not all fears are created equal, there are tools to help you face any fear. For the purposes of this book, I want you to apply these tools to public speaking. But once you have become a courageous speaker, remember you can apply these tools to help you defeat other fears holding you back.

For a long time, I was really hard on myself for making mistakes while speaking. I focused on the audience judging me but all along I was judging myself. You might have experienced the same. I'm here to tell you to cut yourself some slack! To properly karate chop our fears, we are going to focus on two things in this chapter:

1) Your goal is not perfection, your goal is to get in front of people and speak—often.

2) You are going to make mistakes—look forward to them. They will either be your best friend or your worst enemy.

Go ahead and say the following out loud to yourself.

"From this moment on I, [STATE YOUR NAME], give myself permission to suck."

There, I'm glad we got that out of the way. That statement helps lower the expectations that we put on ourselves. It doesn't mean we don't try or don't care. It's actually the opposite but with a twist.

You should want to try hard, do well, and care enough about speaking that you strive for a high standard. However, you also need to understand the importance of leaving room for making mistakes.

Giving yourself permission to suck also helps guide you away from the mindset that mistakes will lead to failure. That viewpoint, taken to extreme levels, can prevent you from even trying altogether.

We want to move away from that initial response to avoid mistakes, and instead, learn to embrace mistakes. This helps us focus on mistakes for what they truly are rather than perceiving them as bad things that we must prevent at all costs.

Once that's clear to you, your viewpoint of the world will start to change. The old you would see an opportunity and ask:

"Is there a chance I could fail?"

That is the wrong question to ask. Of course there is a chance you could fail. That question will stand between your old self and your new self. That question keeps you exactly where you're standing, with no chance of moving forward.

Make your decisions based on a better question:

"Is there a chance for me to grow, expand my comfort zone, face my fears, and/or learn lessons I can use to become a better version of myself?"

That type of question sets you up for success. Answering that question already moves you closer in the direction of your public speaking goals because you will almost always answer with "Yes!" There are hardly any speaking opportunities where you won't expand your comfort zone, face your fears of speaking, and/or learn a lesson through that experience! If you do answer "no," then that opportunity is not for you.

Choosing to ask and answer the second question doesn't leave room for your old self to share his opinion. Since you have given yourself permission to suck, the first question is obsolete. You don't care if you'll suck or not. You care if you'll learn, grow, and/or face your fears.

Sucking or not sucking is not important at this stage. What's important is getting in front of people as much as possible regardless of the outcome.

Which sounds better:

"I spoke in public, failed, and made a lot of mistakes."

Or

"I went out there, tried, and learned a lot of lessons."

The literal words you use have serious power on your attitude and how you approach life. You have a choice to choose the words you will use to describe your experiences, your future opportunities, and your overall outlook on life.

For example the old you might say,

“I wasn’t born for public speaking.”

“I have never been good at speaking, so I never will.”

“I have always been too afraid to speak in front of crowds.”

“It does not matter how much I try, I will never get better.”

This type of self-talk leaves no room for other possibilities. These are lies we tell ourselves, and these lies fall into the category of “safe problems.”

Everyone has a safe problem. We use it as a crutch or excuse as to why we can or can’t do something, whatever that might be. If I believe that I wasn’t born to speak in public, that’s my excuse to justify not speaking in public. I use it to avoid opportunities to speak, or not try my hardest when I’m obligated to speak.

It’s lazy and cowardly. I would know since I used to tell myself the same things. I told myself those statements so many times I truly believed the lies. I drank my own Kool-Aid, so to speak.

It was easier to believe I had an excuse than to put in more effort or accept what I didn’t want to believe. I didn’t want to admit I was a coward. It hurt to admit it. It hurt badly. But eventually, I realized there was no one else to blame but me.

I remember one night in high school when I finally admitted to myself, “I’m truly just a coward” and started to cry. That was a low point for me, but it was the moment of weakness I needed to start finding my greatness, stop making excuses for myself, and start using different words that built me up instead of holding me back.

I was finally willing to accept that I got myself into this mess and I would have to get myself out. In order to accept the mistakes I would make, I had to give myself permission to suck.

Now that you have given yourself permission to suck, you are ready to start slaying this demon. In order to slay this demon, and really any fear, you will need discipline, courage, confidence, principles to follow, and the commitment to take action. So let's talk about how we cultivate those.

CHAPTER 12

DISCIPLINE IS A PUSH

Previously, we dove into what holds us back. Now, we are ready to enter the land of tools, tricks, and concepts that will help us speak in public like the courageous speaker we know we can be. The first concept is my good friend, discipline.

Discipline is the push to do what you know you need to do, even though it might make you feel uncomfortable. It's that faint voice in your head that's trying to get through your thick skull. We've all heard it. Sitting on the couch halfway through a family size bag of cool ranch Doritos while binge watching *The Office*, you catch a glimpse of your running shoes by the door. Your mind drifts back to three months ago when you committed to run three times a week.

You hear a voice in your head say, "I really should go for a run." You know you need to, but you just don't feel motivated to run. Here is the truth about motivation: it's a fickle thing. Motivation is not always there when you really need it. To be honest, it only seems to show up when you are actively doing something you want to do. Right now you are motivated to stay on the couch. You start to have a little pity party for dropping the ball. Then you hear a different voice.

"Work has been tough lately, and I just haven't had the energy to run."

"Today is the first day in weeks I've had time to myself."

"It's chilly outside, and it might rain."

"I might injure myself."

"I can always run tomorrow."

"I worked hard this week and deserve a break, one more day won't hurt me."

Your old self really has a foot in the door now, leading you to feel comfortable pushing off the run for another day. Any reason to stay on the couch and scarf down the rest of those Doritos gets red-carpet treatment into the land of sound reason.

However, you know eventually you will have to recognize that these are simply masked excuses. You shovel in another mouthful of chips to distract yourself from going down that train of thought. . . .

But clear as day, you hear "You made a promise!"

"Remember how you felt three months ago when the elevator broke in the office building at work, and you had to use the stairs to go up two flights of stairs to your floor?"

Thinking back again, you remember struggling to make it up to your floor, huffing and puffing. You made a pit stop in the bathroom, locked yourself in a stall, and started pulling at the collar of your shirt to cool off as you started to sweat. It was embarrassing.

After an extended stay in the stall, you stepped out just to look at yourself in the mirror. You felt angry for letting things go as far as they have. You promised yourself to run three times a week because you never wanted to feel that way again.

The memory almost makes you feel worse. Instead of being encouraged/motivated, it actually makes you want to just forget the whole thing ever happened.

"At least try. Put your shoes on and step outside. If afterwards you still don't want to run, you can come back inside. Deal?"

You figured the simple act of putting on shoes and stepping outside is not a far stretch outside your level of comfort. You brush off the Dorito crumbs from your shirt and make your way to the door. Putting on your shoes makes it crystal clear that they are practically brand new. You've hardly worn them at all since buying them the same day the elevator broke three months ago.

Stepping outside, you immediately feel the chilly wind. Looking around the neighborhood, the cold air wakes you up from the drowsiness caused by hours of snacking and sitting on the couch.

At that moment, you decide you might as well go for a walk since you're already outside. A walk seems harmless enough. At least you'll get a little bit of exercise today. A short walk becomes a long walk, and before you realize it, you've picked up your pace. Walking turns into running, without even much of a thought.

You're sweating profusely. Your joints ache. Your lungs are on fire. Ten minutes of running, and you find yourself wheezing. You stop to catch your breath, and you notice the cold wind cutting your throat as you breathe. The formation of a blister from your new shoes is evident.

You feel awful—but—you can't believe what came from the simple act of putting on your shoes and stepping outside. Smiling, you realize just 20 minutes ago you were accepting defeat. Finally, you thought to yourself, *I can do this!*

All you needed was the discipline to put on your shoes and step outside. Everything else fell into place. After you're already outside with your shoes on, it only takes a little discipline to simply start walking. After that, it only takes a little more discipline to turn walking into running.

However, it takes a lot of discipline to go from sitting on the couch to full on running when you really don't want to. You would need the discipline to go from a place of comfort (sitting on the couch) to a place of discomfort (running, sweating, and exhaustion). In comparison, the discipline to simply put on your shoes is insignificant in comparison. Once that's done, you just need a small morsel of discipline to step outside. Next, let the domino effect continue.

Instead of having the discipline to run three times a week, you just need the discipline to put on your running shoes three days a week. I'm sure you would have no problem convincing yourself to do something so simple.

Putting on your running shoes three days a week soon becomes five days a week. Running for a few minutes becomes a few miles. Those new shoes aren't so new anymore.

After some time, what originally caused you to feel out of breath during that first run is hardly a warmup for you now. Afterwards you feel invigorated and missing a run actually makes you feel noticeably less energetic.

Running hills, in snow, in rain or in the heat of summer are tough mentally and physically, but you have enough endurance built up to carry you through.

Of course you've experienced bumps and bruises and blisters along the way. Tripped a time or two. They might have slowed you down, but they certainly didn't stop you from putting on your shoes the next day.

Facing your fears of public speaking has a very similar approach. You will need the discipline to do the very next step. The discipline needed to speak in front of a crowd on a regular basis seems like a daunting amount, especially if your approach thus far was to stay far away from any chance of having to speak.

However, it doesn't take a lot of discipline to read an affirmation in the morning to help you feel positively about seeking out public-speaking opportunities (we'll talk more about affirmations later in the book). Just like it doesn't take much discipline to put on your running shoes, it doesn't take much discipline to seek public-speaking opportunities. Just like walking didn't take much effort once you were already outside with your shoes on, it only takes a little more discipline to say "Yes" to public-speaking opportunities.

Walking can be compared to showing up to a local public-speaking club like Toastmasters (we'll talk more about Toastmasters later in the book). Since you're already there, you might build up the nerve to do a two minute speech in front of everyone. Now your walk turned into a run, and you didn't even plan for it.

CHAPTER 13

COURAGE IS THE PULL

After implementing the steps in this book, your first speech still may not go well. It could very well be awful, but once it's over, you will think to yourself, *I can do this!*

Discipline is the push and courage is the pull. The two work together to push and pull you toward your better self when you are afraid. Motivation only shows up after you start seeing results, not before. That's why you cannot depend on being motivated to get you through your fears. You need discipline to take the first step and courage to make the next step easier.

Courage is built through taking action to face our fears. Just like you may not have a lot of muscle the first time you start working out, you don't necessarily start off with courage. Over time, your muscles start to grow. Courage is a muscle.

In the beginning, lifting a certain amount of weight might seem difficult. However, building muscle over time makes that same amount of weight easier to lift and move. With courage, what might have seemed terrifying at first becomes less scary over time. If you consistently work at building courage, those terrifying speaking opportunities will be a piece of cake.

There is one catch. Stop running and your endurance will seemingly cease to exist. Stop using your muscles, and your strength will take a hike. Stop using your courage to speak, and it will fade away. Courage is either lost, maintained, or gained. It is not a resource that remains at a constant supply without effort on your behalf.

CHAPTER 14

COURAGE CROSS TRAINING

The steps in this book will help you gain and maintain a healthy dose of courage to truly become a courageous speaker. This courage will certainly carry over to other aspects of your life. Consider building courage while speaking in front of a crowd as cross training for your other goals that you are afraid to pursue.

Usually our fear of trying anything (from my experience) stems from two basic fears:

- Fear of rejection
- Fear of failure

These two fears hit me like a ton of bricks when I first thought about writing this book. Boy, did my coward-self have a heyday as the following thoughts raced through my brain:

- Who would care what I have to say?
- Don't I need to be an "expert" to even consider writing a book in this area?
- I got C's in English in school.
- What if everyone hates my book?
- What if I can't think of enough to even write about?
- Am I too young for people to take me seriously?
- What if I don't even finish and waste a bunch of time and effort for nothing?

I was in a bad state of mind. I could only picture my book on Amazon with several 1 star reviews with people bashing my book, sending my reputation as a speaker down the toilet. I limited my chances of success because I was afraid my book would be a complete failure and people would say it wasn't even worth reading.

My fears got the best of me, which is ironic considering I wanted to write a book about overcoming fears of public speaking. But there I was, drenched in my fears of writing and publishing a book.

That went on for weeks as I really considered giving up on the idea all together. I didn't snap out of that funk until I asked myself out of frustration,

"Why do I even want to write this stupid book??"

I remember sitting in my car stuck in typical Los Angeles traffic, gripping my steering wheel, and verbalizing that question. I sat on that question for a few minutes trying to really uncover why I wanted to write the book. My first thought was "because writing a book sounds cool." It did sound cool, but that was not a great reason to write a book.

I decided to calm down and ask a better question, "Who am I writing this for?" That was an easy question to answer. I wanted to write for anyone who is afraid of public speaking and who wanted to know how to conquer their fears. I wanted to help people determine when their old, coward-self was talking versus when their courageous-self had the floor. Ultimately, I wanted to help more people punch their fears in the face.

It wasn't until then that I finally realized I was letting my fears take control, just like back in high school at the beginning of my journey to becoming a great public speaker. I just had to stop and laugh because I knew what I needed to do to overcome my fears. I must have subconsciously assumed that since I was not getting ready to speak, the techniques I would need to get rid of this fear would be different.

That train of thought was completely wrong. All I needed to do was to have a small amount of discipline to take the first step. Then I would need just a small amount of discipline to take the next step. If I could do that on a consistent basis, I would eventually build enough courage to keep going even if I were afraid.

I've faced my fears before with public speaking, which for me was a bigger fear to conquer compared to writing a book. So, clearly, unless I let myself get in the way, there was no reason I couldn't accomplish this goal. I was being my biggest critic before even writing a single word for this book. I'd already overcome higher mountains. That perspective made my fears of writing seem so small in comparison.

Suddenly, I felt empowered again with all of my experience facing my fears behind me backing me up. Without that, I probably would have just simply given up before I even started. I've done that more times than I would like to count.

I imagine you might have done the same a time or ten. Just like me, you probably thought about doing something, but your coward-self shot down that idea before it could even attempt to take flight. It was immediately deemed too risky due to a chance of failure and cast aside.

You might not have much experience to draw on of consistently facing your fears when attempting something new. Without that foundation to stand on, your coward-self doesn't have to try very hard to pull the rug out from under you.

Now imagine you have consistently faced one of your biggest fears—speaking in public—on a regular basis. Imagine your courageous-self having a voice whenever you attempt to face your fears so now your coward-self is not the only one speaking. It becomes a fight between the two. Since your coward-self only has hypothetical situations of future failures that will most likely never come to pass, it has to fight harder. Your courageous-self has all of your past experience to back him up. Facts are hard to deny. Ultimately, you will have to decide which one to choose.

You get to decide whether your journey will be a stage fight or a stage fright. Let that empower you.

Here, in the Stage Fight Club, there's really only one choice. Hint: it's in the title. ☺

CHAPTER 15

BUILD CONFIDENCE

I chose the title of this chapter very carefully. I kept it short and cut away everything else that I considered non-essential. Two words—two words could almost summarize the entire purpose of this book. It's incredible what can be pulled from such a short phrase, and I would like you to read those two words out loud before diving into the meat of this section. Read them slowly. Slow enough that you start to picture in your head images of what those words bring to mind. Go ahead and do that now.

When I read them slowly, various images came to mind. Yours might be similar or completely different.

Build: I pictured a home starting from a plot of land being built before my very eyes. Day and night flashed by in rapid succession before the home was complete. That quickly morphed into a skyscraper surrounded by large cranes rising higher and higher as the building neared completion.

Confidence: I pictured a man in a business suit giving a quarterly report to a board of directors in a Fortune 500 company. I pictured a young woman leading a community outreach event of 100+

volunteers helping the homeless. I pictured a mechanic elbow deep into the turbine engine of a jet, locating and fixing the source of a major malfunction.

Each word will spark images, formed by pieces of our own life experiences and our perception of the world around us.

By thinking on these two words and the images they conjure, you bring meaning and life to the idea of building confidence.

So let's start with the word "build."

Build is a verb—the action part of the phrase, insinuating that something must be physically done to complete the phrase. We must take action. Action towards whatever we want to build confidence in. Here, in the Stage Fight Club, we want to build confidence in public speaking.

The image that comes to mind when thinking of the word "build" is more often than not something tangible like a home, roads, or you name it.

But now let's look at confidence; it is intangible. You can't touch it, smell it, hear it, or see it. Confidence is not made of matter or energy. It is more an assurance of our ability to perform an action. Confidence is experienced through the results of having it or not having it.

You can't see it as it grows, but you can certainly feel it grow within you over time, but only if you nurture it. In the short term, you may not notice it. Over the long term, you and others will notice that confidence. It is a slow subconscious change; therefore, you can't determine the exact moment your confidence increased.

In a world filled with instant satisfaction, it's all too easy to give up on building anything that takes significant time and effort to notice results.

You will not necessarily notice any improvements right away. However, once you put in the time, the difference between your first speech and one you give after months of consistently building your confidence will be night and day.

However, since these changes are subtle, I have someone record every time I speak. Every few months I'll go back and re-watch my performances compared to my most recent one, and every time I'm surprised by how much I've improved. I highly recommend you do the same.

Building confidence is a personal endeavor. You must take action to build your confidence. No one else can do it for you. You cannot buy it. You cannot watch a video on confidence and build it. You cannot read books about building confidence and build it.

You must literally expend energy and effort into action to build it. Action takes effort and effort is work. In this case, building confidence in public speaking can take a lot of work. Work that might not show results until a significant amount of time has passed. I would argue the amount of time can be seriously shortened by following the steps in this book.

You have to take ownership of building your confidence. That journey is yours. The path is yours to take. The choice to build your confidence is yours to choose.

CHAPTER 16

PRINCIPLES

Everyone has some form of core principles that they live by. These principles have been shaped by how we were raised, the culture we grew up in, what we've been told is truth, and what we've told ourselves over the years of our lives. These principles tend to shape how we go about our day, how we spend our time, the decisions we make, and even how we react to certain circumstances.

You can have simple core principle or belief that breakfast is the most important meal of the day, dogs are great, cats are emotional, and that kale is always gross.

Your principles usually are there to protect you. For example, you might have a core principle that stealing is bad. This helps prevent you from succumbing to the temptation to steal that Shrek 2 soundtrack you've always wanted thus lowering your chances of going to jail.

Over the years I've discovered 7 principles crucial to punch your fears of public speaking in the face. Principles worth reviewing and revisiting from time to time until they are locked inside your skull after you truly believe them.

These fear-punching principles are:

1. Give yourself permission to suck.
2. Running away from your fears actually makes things worse.
3. The only mistake is not trying.
4. It is okay to be nervous.
5. It is not about you.
6. Tell a story.
7. Know your audience is human.

1. GIVE YOURSELF PERMSSION TO SUCK

This principle we've already covered in a previous chapter. As it is one of the first steps toward facing any fear, I decided to dedicate an entire chapter to it.

But it's worth mentioning again to give yourself permission to suck. Make room to make mistakes, learn from them and don't hold yourself to a ridiculous high standard.

2. RUNNING AWAY FROM YOUR FEARS ACTUALLY MAKES THINGS WORSE

It's easy to believe that running away from your fears doesn't cause any harm. Not addressing your fear of speaking won't make a better speaker, but certainly doesn't come with any negative consequences, right?

Wrong.

Every single time we decide to run away, to not face our fears, it's like feeding our inner coward. It's giving you another reason to convince yourself that it is okay to run away. It's okay to hide. To let fear take the lead.

The opportunities you run away from today because you are afraid makes it that much easier to run away again tomorrow. It's a cycle that must be broken to move forward to become your courageous-self.

3. THE ONLY MISTAKE IS NOT TRYING

This principle builds on the first two. Giving yourself permission to suck helps us reframe how we view mistakes. Instead of viewing them as something to be avoided, we can see them for what they truly are: opportunities to learn and improve. Once we believe that, we can realize that there are no true mistakes when we are trying to better ourselves.

However, when we don't even make the attempt to try because we are afraid, that is the only mistake we can truly make. Because that choice has real consequences that we just went over.

4. IT'S OKAY TO BE NERVOUS

It's really easy to mistake nerves for not feeling ready for the task at hand. What one person might call feeling nervous, someone else might call feeling excited. Realize that feeling nervous is not an indicator that you are not good enough. Rather, it means your body is reacting to a circumstance that you take seriously.

5. IT'S NOT ABOUT ME

One of the biggest hurdles of getting over the fear of speaking in front of an audience is the constant focus on ourselves. We just can't seem to stop thinking about how we might mess up, what the audience will think of us, and what might happen to us if we completely bomb.

Combating this inner self negative focus is to look outward. You have to put your focus on something more important. Realize that there might be someone is the audience that could benefit from your message. The moment you do that, you can finally stop focusing on yourself, your mistakes, and your fears. Instead, you can focus on whom your message might impact.

Focusing on benefiting your audience creates a win-win. That helps you stop focusing on how nervous you are and reminds you there is a good chance someone in that crowd will learn from your message. I know for certain you are not going to be able to please everyone, not by a long shot, but something you say or do during your speech will likely resonate with someone in the crowd. It's really difficult to focus on who is going to walk away better off after hearing you speak *and* focus on how afraid you are at the same time.

6. TELL A STORY

Whenever my dad would tell a story, he would always give great details to draw you in. I love listening to my dad because his stories helped me understand what he was saying and relate to him.

It took me longer than it should have to realize how powerful stories are. Stories are important for your audience and for you as a speaker who might be dealing with fears and anxieties.

For your audience, stories can describe situations, aspects, and details that everyone can relate to. They can connect to your audience on a personal level and help them graph what you're trying to get across.

More importantly for the speaker who might be afraid to speak, stories can help us in that area to. Stories from our personal experiences don't have to be memorized like a speech we made from scratch. Those stories are simply recalled from our memory and make it much easier to prepare ahead of time. Secondly, it's difficult to focus on our fears when we are retelling an experience from our past to an audience.

7. KNOW YOUR AUDIENCE IS HUMAN

The first half of that phrase has been tossed around since who knows when: "Know your audience." This means to know your audience well enough to understand what your audience would respond to best.

I took a different approach and extended the phrase to know your audience *is human*. You might ask why I would make that distinction. Sometimes we can forget that our audience is made up of humans. Humans with their own fears, flaws, and insecurities. There is a good chance 90% of your audience is also afraid to speak in public just like you. They aren't a panel of judges ready to throw old food at you and boo you off the stage the moment they smell weakness.

It's actually interesting to hear that your flaws actually help you connect with your audience. No one is perfect, and there isn't much benefit to appearing perfect. Just imagine being in the audience listening to someone brag about themselves, their amazing accomplishments, and how incredible their life is. How likely are you to relate and connect with someone like that? Compare that to a speaker who might be a little nervous and stumble a bit, but they talk about some struggles they've gone through in life, mistakes they've made, and how they overcame those obstacles. Now that would be someone I could connect with. I'm certainly not the greatest of speakers; I've struggled and made plenty of mistakes, so I can look up to someone who overcame obstacles even with their imperfect record.

Another great thing about knowing your audience is human is knowing that they are far more concerned about themselves and their lives than yours. Whether you do great or terrible, chances are your audience will forget all about it 5 minutes after you are done speaking. Humans forget, which means the only person who truly remembers your mistakes is you. No one else really cares. It hurts a bit to think about, but overall it's quite reassuring. It's like knowing that no matter how bad you do, you've got some *Men In Black* technology in your back pocket ready to wipe everyone's memory as soon as you're done speaking.

So how do we put these into practice? You live them. You give yourself room and leeway to make mistakes, you stop running away from what you are afraid of by at least trying, you realize you speaking in front of an audience is not about you or your fears but about the people in your audience who need to hear your message. You incorporate and tell stories in your talks in front of crowds, and you realize your audience is made up of flawed, imperfect humans who are not out to eat you alive.

We've covered how our lives are shaped by our core principles. We then went over the 7 principles for punching your fears of public speaking in the face along with how to put them into practice.

All these principles helped me tremendously in my battle against my fears of public speaking. I hope they help you just as much if not more.

With these principles and through a lot of trial and error, I came up with a process that I've laid out in the following chapters of the book to show you how to punch your fears in the face on a regular basis and win the war.

We're going to talk about the importance of public speaking once a week, how we can accomplish such a task, and best of all how we can have fun doing it. First things first, you'll need to know one thing to get started.

We, here in the Stage Fight Club (there is no rule about not talking about the Stage Fight Club), do not wish to slowly expand our comfort zone. We know life is too short to move slowly. No, we will chase after that future self like it's a hunt by building our lives around punching our fears in the you-know-where. In doing so, we'll put more and more distance between ourselves and our coward-selves daily. Yes, daily!

We know we cannot face our fears and stay within our own level of comfort. We cannot just simply read a book about public speaking to become a better public speaker. We cannot watch a video of a phenomenal speaker and expect to be better speakers by the time the video is over.

In essence, we cannot grow without taking action. This book will not help you unless you put into action what you learn from reading it and actually start public speaking. Like I learned from my experience in Honduras, we have to take action often to maintain that ability. So let's dive in and start becoming a courageous speaker!

SECTION 4

—

HOW TO BECOME A COURAGEOUS SPEAKER

CHAPTER 17

SPEAKING ONCE PER WEEK

If you had the choice between overcoming your fears over a few months versus slowly over 10 years, what would you pick? As little time as possible, right? Who wouldn't? Ten years is a long time to battle fears and anxiety. That's the pull-the-Band-Aid-off-one-arm-hair-at-a-time approach.

We here in the Stage Fight Club are hard core and don't even use Band-Aids, but if we did, we'd rip them off like greased lightning.

When I decided I was going to get over my fear of speaking, I simply determined I would speak in front of a crowd at least once a week to overcome my fears as fast as possible. More than once a week would accelerate my growth, but at least once a week was a good baseline.

And, of course, before you speak you must practice, which gives you daily practice. Practice is going to be one of the biggest determining factors in your success, and we all know what it looks like when someone doesn't put the necessary time in to prepare.

No boss wants to go to a quarterly meeting and have his employees wing it while they try briefing on how the last quarter went.

No congregation wants to go to church to hear a preacher wing his message on stage. That goes double for the choir.

No one pays to go to a comedy club to watch a comedian who didn't prepare their jokes, stories, or punchlines.

No one wants to listen to a keynote speaker who decided they would make it up as they go.

No one wants to hear the best man give a speech that was not prepared.

No one wants to be taught by a teacher who did not prepare a lesson plan.

Practice goes hand-in-hand with overcoming our fears and anxieties as we keep moving forward to become our better selves. So not only will we practice speaking in public once a week, but we will practice daily for the event, maintaining and nurturing our skills even more.

I'll show you the many ways you can get in front of a crowd once a week later in this book. For now we'll stick with the *why* and we'll save the *how* for later.

You: Will that really be enough to overcome my fears?

Absolutely! That's 52 additional public speaking events you probably would not have intentionally sought after. Do you think you would be a different person after 52 speeches in a year? I guarantee you will. There's no way not to be after that. However, it won't take you the whole year to notice a change. Four weeks is enough time to notice serious changes.

Plus, teaching offers one huge advantage compared to a lot of other careers: you get the summer off. I understand your summers are still filled with responsibilities, secondary jobs, teaching summer school classes, etc. However, having the summer months off from teaching school allows you to focus on other task such has punching your fears of public speaking in the face on a weekly basis.

Now that you have committed to speak once a week, you're now ready to hear what it takes to prepare to speak once a week in the next chapter.

CHAPTER 18

IMPORTANCE OF COMMITTING AN HOUR A DAY

After reading the title to this chapter you might be think, an hour a day? I hardly feel there's enough time in the day as it is. How do I add this to my life without it affecting something else?

I would definitely expect it to affect your current life. If you are having a hard time even considering an hour a day, then you are not that serious about overcoming your fear of public speaking. That's the old you talking, and he is trying hard to find reasons to keep things the way they are.

The old you will say anything to make sure life doesn't change. Change is typically uncomfortable for most people, especially change that puts a strain on our current comfort level. However, we cannot grow within the confines of a routine because nothing changes. If nothing changes, our lives are stagnant. I'm not saying routines are bad, but we can't expect things to change within a routine, and it would be insanity to think otherwise.

My question to you is, "Is it worth it?" Is it honestly worth living in fear and living with anxiety over speaking in public if you don't have to?

Would you not gladly dedicate an hour a day to relieve yourself of your fears and stressors that do nothing but cause you unnecessary grief and hold you back from your true potential? Why settle for a second-class version of yourself if you already have what it takes to become a better you? The only thing stepping in the way of your better self is time and effort. Those are small prices to pay for what's ahead.

So choose to change. Choose to take the risk and face your fears daily.

Fear will either hinder you, or it will simply be an obstacle. Your choice.

Fear will stop you from taking a chance on a business opportunity.

Fear will cut you down when all you want to do is apply for that professors' job at your alma mater.

Fear will hold you back from running for a leadership position in the committee you're involved in.

Fear will stop you from even trying.

Fear will either stop you or make you a better person. The choice is 100% yours, but only if you take responsibility for your life. The moment you don't take responsibility for your life is the moment you give your choice to someone or something else.

Imagine facing one of the decisions mentioned above after a year of speaking in public once a week and practicing daily. Take showing up to an interview for that professor position you applied for, for example: That nervous, uncomfortable feeling in your stomach when you are about to do something that matters is far from foreign to you by now. It's that feeling of approaching what you are afraid of instead of running from it. By now you've built up a tolerance to it.

You've grown to live with it, and you even use it to perform at your best as your body releases small doses of adrenaline to keep you at your peak performance. This feeling isn't new to you. The old you might peek his head in and whisper, "what if. . ." before walking in, but you have heard that song so many times now that you drive in without slowing your pace. You step through the threshold and take a moment to think back one year's time and realize how far you've come.

Without that practice, you might have chosen to never apply for the job in the first place. You might have convinced yourself that now is not a good time. There's probably other candidates more qualified for the job who have applied and the chances of getting hired are slim since you don't have any experience teaching at a university.

But you do have that practice behind you, and you can face your fears head on and enter that interview knowing you'd be a great fit for the job.

Even after understanding the importance of committing this time, it can still seem daunting. Just realize you can get creative. Most of the tasks throughout the week can be done during a lunch break. You can even rehearse your speech during your commute to and from work or while running errands.

If I'm waiting in a public place for whatever reason and I have time to rehearse, I will rehearse. However, just so I don't get weird looks for "talking to myself," I'll pull out my phone and act as though I'm talking to someone. I'll even visualize myself in front of the crowd if I'm just sitting around doing nothing.

You: Can I just do all of this the day before if I have the time?

Yes, it's definitely possible but you will be missing out on the most important aspect of this approach: daily and consistent practice. Doing everything the day before prevents you from making public speaking, and ultimately facing your fears, a part of your daily life.

Working every day toward your goal of facing your fears has far more benefits in the sense of growth dividends compared to simply preparing only the day before. Also, if something comes up the day before and you can't get everything done, you've put yourself in an awful situation of going in blind so to speak.

CHAPTER 19

START YOUR PLAN WITH AFFIRMATIONS

Now that you are committed and ready, let's get into the real meat of our plan. I want to warn you that a plan is only good if you actually put it into action. If you don't actually follow through because of [insert excuse here], then everything prior to this is wasted.

You have to commit to follow through with action prior to writing your plan. It's too easy to feel like you accomplished something just by spending the time making a plan. But having a plan is negligible compared to what you gain from taking the first step. So make a firm commitment now before we get started. Say the following out loud:

I, [state your name], commit to put my plan into action. I know a plan without action is useless, and *doing* is far greater than *planning*.

Now if you just read over that and didn't verbalize it, then hike your eyes back up there and let's try that again. You're only cheating yourself. Say it out loud a few times even. If you did read out loud the first time, then move on.

Verbalizing your plan is just as important as rehearsing your speech out loud. If you just rehearse it in your head, you will not perform as well. Rehearsing out loud also adds sensory data to your memory and experience, causing you to focus on the pronunciation of every word and actually hear what you are saying. These additional steps add more layers of information to your practice and have a greater effect on your memory due to the increased feedback.

That's the importance of saying the above statement out loud because the impact is far greater and has a better chance of sticking in your mental capacity versus just reading it in your head. For good measure, let's say it out loud one more time. If you want to add fuel to the fire, say it with conviction.

I, [state your name], commit to put my plan into action. I know a plan without action is useless, and *doing* is far greater than *planning*.

With that out of the way, plan for your plan to suck. It will most likely change. Every plan seems perfect until you put it into action because plans hardly ever match reality. We'll do our best to make our plan to speak once a week, but it's better to know ahead of time that things will not always go accordingly.

Life happens and you might not get to practice like you planned, or speak every single week, or you name it. Expect this to happen ahead of time so you don't get blindsided or discouraged and end up giving up. Every plan will face bumps, bruises, and obstacles, but remember those are simply life's way of giving feedback.

It's time to write down a plan. Go ahead and grab something to write with and write on. I'll wait.

You're ready? Cool. At the top, write "Speaking Plan." Right under that, write down the following affirmation that you will recite once in the morning and in the evening before bed:

"From now on, I will be on the hunt for opportunities to speak. No longer will I run away when an opportunity crosses my path, letting fear and my coward-self win. When opportunity knocks on my door, I will immediately say, "Yes!" before my old, coward-self has a chance to scream, "No!" Throughout the day, I will continuously remind myself 'I, [state your name], will become a courageous speaker.'"

Now affirmations are one of those weird things that shouldn't work, but they do . . . internally at least. It's not like you can continuously tell yourself, "I'm going to be a millionaire. I'm going to be a millionaire. I'm going to be a millionaire," and the world will bend toward your will to make that a reality. The world doesn't change because of what you tell yourself, but *your* world certainly can because you are choosing what is important in *your* world.

This is a form of reticular activation—a small portion of the brain that acts like a night club bouncer responsible for letting important information in and keeping the unimportant information out. For example, when you're in a crowded room and everyone's talking to one another, you can't make out what anyone in particular is saying, but out of the white noise, you can hear someone say your name. Why? Because your name is the most important word in *your* world. You've already deemed that word important so picking that out of the noise is literally a no-brainer.

That's kind of how affirmations work. Continuously telling yourself "I will hunt down and seek out opportunities to speak throughout my day" does not automatically create opportunities. This simply changes the lens you see your life through. Opportunities now become important, and your brain will stop filtering them out.

As you start to do this, opportunities will seemingly pop out of nowhere, but they were always there to begin with. There's just a high chance you weren't looking for them. In reality, you were probably avoiding them.

The second portion of the affirmation will be your daily mantra: "I, [state your name], will become a courageous speaker." Say this out loud three times in a row every time you say it.

At first, you may forget to say it throughout the day, but it will soon become a normal part of your day. I've used several methods to help me remember, and the best way is to have a reminder that grabs your attention throughout the day. I've taken a plastic duck and taped it to a pen I use in my office. Every time I go to use it I ask myself, "Why did I do that? Why did I tape a duck to this pen?" That's when I remember to say my affirmations. Sounds ridiculous, but ridiculous is what I needed to prevent my brain from filtering out my reminder. Use whatever you need to help you remember throughout the day.

I also like to tape my morning affirmation to my car's steering wheel and on my bathroom mirror so I have no choice but to see it and remember to say my affirmation.

You: I'm game with looking for opportunities, but I'm still not seeing the point of telling myself I will become a courageous speaker. Seems pointless to me.

It would probably help to let you in on a little secret. You already use affirmations. You've been using them for a long time. However, they've most likely been negative affirmations. Little lies you tell yourself that you have gradually started to believe. These lies don't serve you. They feed your lesser self. Some of the following negative affirmations you might know all too well:

"I'm just not good enough to speak and probably never will be."

"I'm not talented like other speakers."

"No one cares what I have to say."

"There's no point trying because I'm not going to get any better."

"I always screw up and make mistakes in front of a crowd."

"I am a failure."

If you tell yourself something long enough, you are not only going to start believing the lie, but your brain will notice incidents supporting your beliefs and filter out anything contrary to your worldview.

It's been said that our attitude, expectations, and outlook on life are directly affected by the accumulation of our thoughts. If our thoughts are just riddled with negative affirmations about how much we suck at public speaking and how there's no changing that "fact," then it is hard to believe our thoughts could change or manipulate the way we approach public speaking, but they can.

Since our thoughts have such an effect on our lives, why not use them to our advantage to punch our fears in the face? Why not make them positive and empowering thoughts that better serve ourselves? We've already talked about how the words we use are important. Now we're going to use our thoughts to push us forward to look for opportunities to speak instead of holding us back.

Speaking of looking for opportunities to speak. . .

CHAPTER 20

ON THE HUNT

With our thoughts in check, after stating our affirmation out loud, we are now on the hunt for opportunities to speak. Any experienced hunter will hunt in locations that increase their odds. If deer is on the menu, then the woods is the place to be, and probably a section of woods where deer have been spotted before.

We'll take the same approach while looking for an opportunity to speak. We'll start by looking in places where people speak regularly.

Toastmasters

First things first, let's hop on our handy dandy laptop or smartphone and look up local Toastmasters' clubs in our area. I mentioned Toastmasters earlier in the book, so I'll briefly explain what it is for those who don't know. Toastmasters is an international club where members gather weekly to give prepared speeches or short, unprepared speeches called table topics for the sole purpose of developing its members into great and confident communicators and leaders. Toastmasters also hosts several speech competitions throughout the year, which is a phenomenal arena to supercharge our path to becoming a courageous speaker.

If the idea of competing scares the poop out of you, that might be a great sign that competing is exactly something you should considering doing.

Toastmasters can become a one-stop shop to satisfy our one speech a week requirement. It is one of the only places where your audience is there to help you succeed because they are there for the same reason you are: to become a better speaker. It's a safe environment to practice, make mistakes, and get better on a weekly basis.

Keep in mind Toastmasters is not free. Now, before you put the padlock on your wallet, I'm here to tell you it's beyond worth it. While I'm a frugal guy who typically cringes at spending anything over $5 on non-essential items, especially on something such as a club membership, this investment has been well worth it.

It is only $50 for six months. That's less than $10 a month to be among a group of people helping me punch my fears in the face and willingly be my audience every week. That's a bargain, and the value is priceless.

Some of us have spent thousands on furthering our education and most of us spend more than Toastmasters' fees with a few visits to Starbucks. The money is negligible compared to what you can get out of it.

While there are other places to hunt for opportunities, this is my first go to source. I simply shoot an email to the VP of our club requesting to speak at the upcoming club meeting. If there is an opening, I've got my speaking gig lined up for the week.

With regards to competing, winning at each level (club, area, and division) allows you to keep competing all the way to district, guaranteeing you have to give a speech every week as you are either competing or practicing at the weekly club meetings. The first competition I competed in gave me eight weeks of speaking opportunities. Not bad.

I hope by now I've got you seeing the value in Toastmasters because now you need to find a local club near where you live or work. This can be as simple as going on www.meetup.com and searching "Toastmasters" or going on www.toastmasters.org and finding a club near you.

You: Well, Cody, I looked, and there isn't a club around me for 100 miles. What do I do now?

You've got two options: start your own Toastmasters club in your area or look someplace else to speak weekly. Starting a club in your area is a tough task, but that alone can supercharge your ability to speak as well as further your leadership abilities. The scope of that is beyond the context of this book, but don't let that discourage you from considering starting a club.

For the rest of our time in this section, I will show you plenty of other places you can give your weekly speech.

Work

Just look where you spend the better part of your day: work. Odds are in your favor that you will have opportunities to speak there. After all, there's bound to be annual or monthly training everyone has to take. There is safety training, ethics training, emergency evacuation training, so on and so on. The trainings never seem to end, or so it seems. That's great news for you! Someone has to instruct or teach those trainings and, most likely, a poor soul just got assigned this extra duty. If that's the case, then they would be more than willing to give that additional duty to you if you request it.

Since you are probably teaching at a school, I can only imagine the number of school events the schools host throughout the year. Several of those events require an emcee. You could be the go-to emcee for these school events.

Participate in faculty meetings or committee meetings in a way that requires you to speak.

Get involved with leading a local/regional teaching workshop.

Talk to your forum leader about speaking at a teacher forum.

Speak at a Professional Learning Communities (PLC).

Talk to your district personal to volunteer to speak at District In-Services.

Talk to your principal or PTA president to speak at the PTA meetings.

Present your ideas or research at a teaching convention. Talk to the meeting planner of any particular convention to grab a speaking slot.

Talk to the Induction Coordinator to speak at mentor meetings or induction teacher meetings.

Talk to the teacher responsible for the teacher cadet program to speak at the teacher cadet forum.

Talk to the faculty member over the Future Teachers of America Club in your school district to speak to the students about your experience as a teacher.

Church

If you happen to go to church, there are tons of opportunities to speak. You can lead a morning Bible study. Teach a Sunday school lesson to children. Give the service prayer before or after the sermon. My church has an individual speaker at the end of a Sunday sermon to give a weekly status of events and things to come over the next couple of weeks.

Funny enough, my pastor read my first book and requested I start giving the weekly status update.

Guest Speaker

One thing to consider is being a guest speaker at different venues in your own community. Two my top favorite are the following:

1) Most communities have local Rotary Clubs, Chamber of Commerce, and Young Professional Organizations. All of these groups need speakers for their weekly or monthly meetings throughout the year. So find someone you know who is a member and ask them if their group is looking for speakers and what topics they typically look for.

2) Odds are in your favor that a college, university, or even technical centers are close to where you live. Some professors or instructors love having guest speakers come in and talk to their class on a related subject.

Common Interest Groups

Have an interest or hobby you love to talk about? Are you into bee keeping? Needlepoint? Programming phone apps? Do you have some mad nunchuck skills? If so, then do a Google search or check in with social media accounts to find groups with similar interests near you and volunteer to speak to the group. This will be an easy talk to put together since you have an interest in the topic.

Network

Reach out to your network to find more opportunities to speak. Post on Facebook if anyone knows of an opportunity to speak. Ask your fellow teachers, the principal, your pastor, or your community leaders the same thing. Be genuine in your request by telling them exactly what you're doing by looking for opportunities to become a better speaker by punching your fears in the throat. People are more open when you can be upfront about your intentions. Just don't threaten to punch them in the throat.

Improv Groups

To supercharge my growth, I'll look for opportunities to speak or perform on stage in front of an audience where I can't prepare ahead of time what I'm going to say or do. I'm forced to think on my feet.

I mentioned before that Toastmasters has 2 minute table topics where you are given a random topic to speak on for—you guessed it—2 minutes.

I also like to go on www.meetup.com and look up local improv groups that meet up on weekends. Originally, I never considered joining an improv/acting group. However, one week over the summer, I didn't have a chance to speak at all, so I figured I'd do a little Google search.

I couldn't really find anything that I would typically go to, but a local improv group caught my attention. The thoughts of improvisation actually made me feel uncomfortable. I was actually a little afraid to show up and give it a shot—so that's exactly what I did. I showed up and gave it a shot. ☺ It was great, I had fun, and it got me out of my comfort zone.

Create your own opportunities

There's no reason you cannot create opportunities to speak for yourself. If starting a Toastmasters Club seems too daunting, then go on to www.meetup.com and start a casual public speaking group in your community. There are bound to be more people looking for a place to become a better speaker. You can be the person to create it. If anything, you could create a group that meets at work in the mornings or during lunch for the sole purpose of improving everyone's public speaking skills.

Do you like board games? Did you know there is a board game to help you improve your public speaking? Two of my fellow Toastmasters, Florian Mueck and John Zimmer, actually developed and manufactured a public-speaking game called *Rhetoric – The Public Speaking Game* that also comes in an app version. The board game itself is a little on the pricey end, and it has to ship from Europe. Luckily the app is only $6.99 as of writing this, which is a great price to have a fun time hanging out with friends and improving your public speaking at the same time. If you are somehow able to squeeze this game into a lesson plan, even better. You and your students can improve your public speaking skills at the same time.

—Cody's Note—

If you are considering purchasing the physical board game, you can reach out to the creators here: www.rhetoricgame.com.

Remember, you are looking for one opportunity to speak each week. Shoot for speaking for at least five minutes and try to find speaking opportunities that require you to prepare a speech ahead of time.

Speaking once a week is the goal, but life happens so don't fret too much. If a week or two goes by, and you haven't had the chance to speak, just make sure you are consistently saying your affirmation and always be on the lookout for opportunities.

Your opportunities can come from a combination of what I've mentioned above, which is certainly not an all-inclusive list by any means. From Toastmasters, work, Church, volunteering, and your network, you are very likely to find opportunities to speak.

Now add to your plan, writing down at least five places you could look for opportunities to speak. Let those be your hunting ground. Now go out there and look for opportunities, ask for opportunities, and create some if you have to. Before you know it you'll have more opportunities than you know what to do with.

Get ready to accept . . .

CHAPTER 21

WHEN OPPORTUNITY KNOCKS

When you are on the hunt for an opportunity to speak and an opportunity presents itself, typically, you would think about the opportunity then act on it afterwards. However, that creates too much time for your coward-self (the old you) to interject with a mountain of reasons why you can't or shouldn't take them up on the opportunity to speak.

While you are in the middle of mentally flipping through your calendar, your old self will chime in with something like:

"That's just another thing to add to my plate, and I'm busy as it is."

"Eight at night? That's way too late in the night to speak! Especially on a weeknight!"

"There is someone else who could speak on this better than me."

The comments will be never-ending, and the more time you take to think about it, the more uncomfortable you will feel, and the more likely you will decline the opportunity.

I want you to be hungry for an opportunity to speak and jump for it like it's a cheeseburger (or a pile of kale if you're vegan) and you haven't eaten for eight days. I want you to accept before your coward-self has time to even know what hit him.

You want to stop going to a place of fear and stress when an opportunity presents itself, but instead go immediately to a place of excitement.

This is why the morning affirmation is so important! Reading it out loud in the morning sets the tone for the day. Instead of falling into the same trap of avoiding and declining a chance to speak, you are now telling yourself (with conviction!) to look for a chance to speak first thing in the morning.

Don't forget about your daily mantra to become a courageous speaker. A courageous speaker jumps at an opportunity to speak even if the opportunity is terrifying. A courageous speaker does NOT listen to their coward-self and the laundry list of reasons why they should run like hell instead.

You: "But what if I accept an opportunity to speak, but later realize I truly can't due to circumstances outside of my control?"

I would rather have you politely decline after accepting than to take time to think about the opportunity and eventually talk yourself out of it. If you TRULY have circumstances outside of your control that prevent you from speaking, then that's perfectly understandable.

However, if the reason you cannot speak has a flavor of inconvenience, or not making time for it, or not feeling comfortable, then that's just making excuses.

I've fallen into this trap myself. Many times I've had to have some serious talks with myself about why I couldn't speak. I've found myself coming up with some pretty lame excuses that I truly wanted to believe were outside of my control, but they were not.

I didn't want to accept that I was the one making the decision to be a coward. Accepting that would mean having to take responsibility for my actions or inaction in this case. Looking deeper, my excuses all stemmed from my fears. I have worked to overcome that, and you need to too. Choose to say "yes" rather than "no."

Once you get in that habit, I would love to say your coward-self crawls back into his cave and shuts up, but that is typically far from reality. Your acceptance will most likely come across as disrespect to His Lowliness, The Coward King.

"What were you thinking!?" the Coward King yells as soon as he receives word you betrayed him. The answer, of course, is you were not thinking at all for once. An opportunity came knocking, and finally you opened the door without giving it a second thought.

But now the lowly king will feel blindsided, furious even, and he'll do whatever is in his power to make you second guess what you've just done. Even going as low as bringing up past memories of your "failures" speaking in front of an audience, but luckily you have already addressed those memories by turning those failures and mistakes into lessons.

The Coward King will be furious, but he will eventually grow tired, give up and become silent.

Every now and then leading up to the time for you to speak, he'll try again to convince you to retreat. Change is hard, but stay strong. Expect the Coward King to speak up, and it won't catch you by surprise. It will get easier and easier to recognize his voice in your head, which in turn will make it easier to tune him out.

CHAPTER 22

I SAID YES, NOW WHAT??

If you have a speaking opportunity coming up, it's now time to prepare for your big speech. So you're going to use the other six days of the week to prepare and use as your playground to hone your skills.

If on Wednesday, you scheduled to speak next Tuesday then consider Wednesday day one.

Keep in mind this plan assumes you have at least seven days to prep for your speech. If you have more time to prepare, ranging greater than two weeks, I highly encourage you to find more opportunities to speak in the coming weeks prior to the opportunity at hand.

If you can't find another chance to speak, your once a week goal can be easily accomplished by simply preparing as if your speech is only 7 days away. For example, if you have two weeks between now and when you actually speak, go through the steps we are about to address during the first week, and at the end of the week, speak in front of friends, family, and/or co-workers as a dry run. Gather feedback from your practice audience, incorporate any needed improvements in yourself or your speech content, and then use the following week to simply practice giving your speech daily leading up until your actual speech day.

However, if your speech is greater than 30 minutes, then use all two weeks to work on it rather than the dry run method. It is still possible to properly prepare within six days, but your goal is to minimize the amount of time needed to prepare each day. If your speech requires more time to prep, then you will simply repeat days two through four until the last two days prior to speaking.

—Cody's Note—

If you have less than a week to prepare, then skip to chapter 24 where I talk about what to do in those situations.

DAY 1

On day one, you need to get your act together. If you don't already know your topic, then that's Step 1. Most speaking events at work or in community involvement will give a good idea of the topic.

However, your speech might be for a public speaking group like Toastmasters or a local meet-up where the topic of your speech is completely up to you, and you'll have to start from scratch.

After deciding on the topic, you will spend the first day creating content, structuring your speech, and creating a rough draft.

Note: If you already have prepared content for your speech, skip to day two.

Be sure to carve out an hour of your day to complete the following steps:

Step 1: Know your topic
Step 2: Mind map
Step 3: Outline your speech
Step 4: Rough draft

Step 1: Know Your Topic

Note: If you already know your topic but need content, skip this step.

Try not to take more than 10 minutes to come up with a topic. Choose something you have experience with or a personal story you can connect to the topic. Having a story will make it easier to come up with content, though this is not essential.

Remember, our goal is not to deliver superior content, awe our audience, nor to be remembered as a legendary orator. All those things are great, worthy goals. However, we are working towards overcoming our fears and becoming more and more comfortable in front of a crowd. It truly doesn't matter how superior your content is if you are terrified to speak. The goal is to have the courage to get in front of a crowd. Keep that in mind and don't put too much pressure on finding the perfect topic.

With that in mind, let's say you looked around the room and noticed a bowl of fruit, particularly a bundle of delicious looking bananas, and you thought to yourself, "Boy, do I love bananas." Then choose bananas as your topic. Step 1 complete. Nailed it.

Yes, I realize this is an extreme case of truly not caring what your topic is, but let's roll with it.

Step 2: Mind Mapping

You might remember mind-mapping from grade school. You wrote your topic in the middle and branched off that topic to connect and write down everything you could think of. This is used a lot as a brainstorming activity to help you get everything out of your brain and onto paper. It's going to look messy, but messy is fine.

Now I want you to do this with me. Take no longer than 10 minutes and begin creating a mind map for the bananas topic.

If you haven't done this before or haven't for a long time, I'd like to share with you some expert level advice: Write down ANYTHING that comes to mind and don't hold anything back. Your mind naturally starts judging or filtering thoughts as you go through the exercise because they seem silly or unrelated or stupid. All ideas are good ideas. Any thought that comes to your mind might not seem related or useful, but write it down anyway because that thought might spur a connection to something else related or useful, or remind you of a past experience/memory that will open up a whole gambit of content to speak on.

When you are ready, get out a blank sheet of paper and get to mind mapping! Try not to take more than 10 minutes.

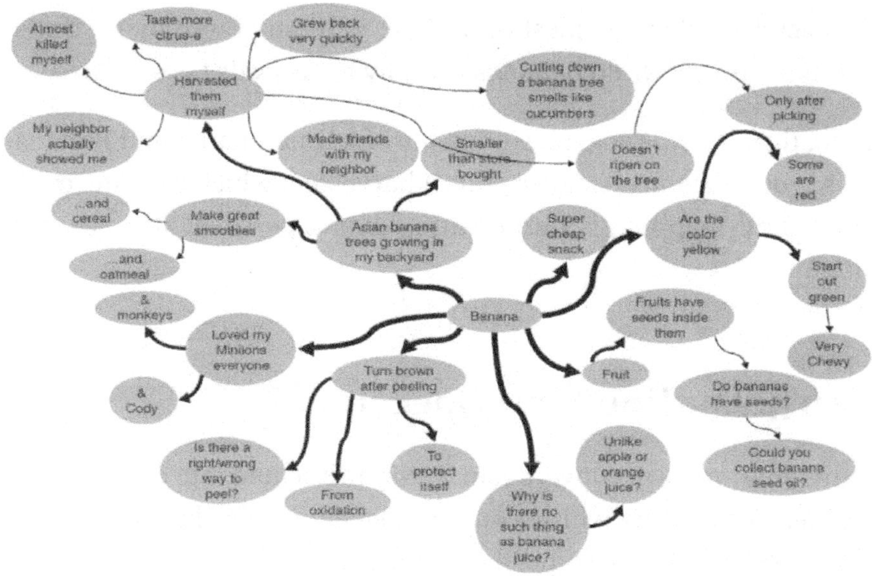

As you can see from my example, I have main branches off the main topic, and then I have even more branches off those main branches as I went through the exercise. This took me a grand total of four minutes to complete, and I had enough to talk about for at least 20 minutes. Luckily, we only need 5–7 minutes of content. With just four minutes of effort, I have more than I need. Now that's a good problem to have.

Don't be discouraged if it takes you longer to complete your mind map. Like all things, public speaking included, it gets easier with practice.

As you can see from my mind map, I wrote everything that came to mind. I wrote down things as simple as bananas are the color yellow, which spurred on more branches about how they start out green and how they don't actually ripen on the tree but only ripen after picking. Bananas also reminded me of the Minions from the animated movie *Despicable Me*.

The exercise led me to question wonder why isn't there such a thing as banana juice? Or do bananas actually have seeds?

Going through this also reminded me of a time I had Asian Banana trees growing in my backyard that I harvested, which gave me even more mind-mapping material since I had a personal story to talk about.

Step 3: Outline Your Speech

In this step, you will convert your messy mind map into a less messy outline. The outline will become the structure or skeleton of our banana speech. I took some of my main branches and used them as my main subtopics. Anything that branched off my main branches, I wrote underneath as a subtopic and so on and so forth.

Banana Speech Outline:

1. Bananas are the color yellow
    a. Some are red
        i. Do they taste different?
    b. Start out green
        i. Very chewy when they are green
    c. Bananas don't actually ripen on the tree
        i. Only after picking off the tree
    d. Turn brown after peeling
        i. Due to oxidation
        ii. To protect itself
    e. Is there a right and wrong way to peel a banana?
2. Bananas are a fruit
    a. Fruits have seeds inside them
        i. Do bananas have seeds?
        ii. Is it possible to collect banana seed oil?
    b. Why is there no such thing as banana juice?
        i. Like apple and orange juice?
3. Story about my Asian Banana Trees

a. Harvested them myself after my neighbor showed me how
    i. Tastes more citrusy than store bought
    ii. Smaller too
    iii. Great in smoothies, cereal or oatmeal
b. Almost killed myself harvesting
    i. About fell off a ladder
c. The trees grow back quickly
    i. The trees start to bleed when you cut them down
    ii. The banana tree blood smells like cucumbers
        1. Very sticky and will stain your clothes

4. ETC
    a. Bananas are loved by Minions everywhere
        i. & Cody
        ii. & monkeys
    b. Super cheap snack

After I converted everything over to my outline, I organized the topics in order.

This took me roughly 10 minutes to complete.

You might have noticed I added more under some of the subtopics than what was on my mind map. Converting my mind map over to my outline helped me remember even more content, so I wrote those new ideas down.

If you are a perfectionist, like myself, do your best to fight the urge to make your outline perfect from the get-go. Go ahead and convert your banana mind map over to your outline if you haven't already. This can be done on a different sheet of paper or on the back of the sheet of paper you wrote your mind map on.

Step 4: Rough Draft

There are several ways to write your rough draft. One method can save you time: Use a computer to convert what you say into text. There is some pretty expensive software out there that can do this for you . . . or you can do it for free. ☺

With your outline in front of you, complete these steps:

Step 1) Open up a web browser using *Chrome*.

Step 2) Go to www.google.com and type in: Web speech API Demonstration.

Step 3) Open the "Web Speech API Demonstration - Google" link.

Step 4) Click the microphone icon on the next screen and just simply start speaking on your topic, using your outline to guide you.

—Cody's Note—

You can also insert punctuation using your voice: say "Period" or "Comma" to insert those marks or say "New paragraph" to go to a new paragraph.

Again, don't try and make it perfect the first go around. Just speak because this is a draft, not a final product. Consider it more of a prototype.

The reason this is so effective is because we can speak SO MUCH faster than we can type or write free hand. It won't be even close to perfect, but you can edit later. Cut yourself some slack and get to speaking!

This took me roughly 10 minutes to open up a web browser and talk through my entire outline. 10 minutes and BOOM! My rough draft is complete!

I'll take a few more minutes to make soft edits if words are missing or if the software didn't pick up on a sentence or two. Other than that I'm done for the day.

All four steps should take less than an hour to complete, even if you have to type out and/or hand write your speech.

At this point, you haven't spoken a single word as far as practicing goes, and that's okay. If you try cramming more into your day, then it is easy to start associating practice, preparing, and learning with a lot of time and effort. Once that happens, Netflix starts looking even more enticing compared to practicing.

Don't get me wrong: It is a lot of time and effort. Here, in the Stage Fight Club, we don't believe in lying, and I'm not going to start lying to you. Since you made it this far into the book (I congratulate you for getting this far!), you already know and accept that it does take a lot of time and effort to overcome your fears. However, that doesn't mean you can't spread out that time and effort over a week.

With the rough draft complete, pat yourself on the back! You just got a lot of work done, and it's only day one. On Day 2, you'll actually start practicing and editing your speech as it really starts to take shape.

DAY 2

Day two, you will actually begin rehearsing your speech. Just know that this will be a rough, rough draft. Some people want to try and perfect their speech on paper before actually doing a dry run.

If this is your first time going through this, you should have your banana rough draft ready to go.

Before you start, reassure yourself that you are working with a rough, rough draft of your speech. Reading through it, you may think, *good gracious, this is horrible,* and you'll probably be right.

In its current state, it is probably very bad, but I want you to remember that this is all part of the plan. The final draft will be much better. The speech you actually give to your audience compared to your draft will feel like night and day. With that mindset ready, let's begin.

Have your speech in front of you and speak every word from beginning to end. As you read, just make mental notes of the flow of your speech.

When you are done, speak through it again, and this time make written notes of choppy sentences, sections that need more clarity, sections that should probably be removed, and needed transitions to create better flow from one idea to the next.

I like to print out my draft and make edits with a red pen. I'll read through the draft several times, and each time I'll pick up more and more that I want to change, edit, remove, or add to chisel away at my draft. I'll spend 20–40 minutes doing this. Saying it out loud helps you edit your draft and will start stimulating mental roots in your brain to help you memorize your speech.

After you are feeling more comfortable with your revised draft (it's still a draft so it should not be perfect!), you are ready to try and video record yourself on either your phone, digital camera, or laptop.

—Cody's Note—

If you don't have a way to record yourself, ask a friend who has a phone, camera, or laptop you can borrow for this part. If that simply is not possible, just practice giving your speech out loud in private a few times in front of a mirror.

With your recording device up and running, do your best to remember your content, but don't worry if you need to look at your written speech; this is all just practice.

If you mess up during your recording, try not to start over. Keep chugging along as if nothing happened. In front of an audience, you won't get the opportunity to just start over, so this is perfect practice to mess up and keep moving along as if nothing happened. Remember, your audience will not remember your mistakes.

Once you're done recording, watch yourself give your speech. It can be VERY uncomfortable to watch yourself. It certainly is for me even though I've done it hundreds of times. However, this will give you some of the best feedback you will ever receive. Most speakers don't do this, and it's a shame. This simple exercise reveals so much about ourselves that we don't even realize. For me, I noticed little quirks to indicate nervousness; incorrect pronunciations; and my voice trailing off at the end of sentences, making it hard for my audience to hear.

Watching yourself speak can be an uncomfortable eye opener, but a priceless way to learn and improve! Don't downplay the importance of this step simply because it's awkward or uncomfortable.

As you are watching your recording ask yourself the following questions:

Are you smiling?

How's your tone of voice?

Do you have vocal variation or are you mostly monotone?

Did your speech flow smoothly from one topic to the next?

Did each topic have enough clarity to make sense to your audience who might not have the same knowledge or background as you?

What are your hands doing?

What does your body language say about how you are feeling?

Do you look uncomfortable?

Did you display signs of a nervous tick?

Write down what you could improve in a notebook. Reflect on how you did and what you could do better. I do this with all of my speeches, and even after doing this hundreds of times, I still find things I could do better.

Professionals in any field don't reach professional status because they know everything there is to know in their field. They become professionals because they never stopped learning and improving.

So don't feel discouraged if you find a lot to improve on, and definitely don't expect to fix everything over night! For now, pick two or three things from your notes to focus on during the remainder of today's practice time. Continue to record, make notes, and then practice.

—Cody's Note—

If you already had content (like pre-made slides) for your speech, then complete day two twice: today and tomorrow. Try to practice without looking at your slides. Afterwards go through the other steps for Day 2: recording yourself, watching the recording, noting feedback, and then practice again.

DAY 3

Today give your speech in front of someone. That's right! Get ready to speak in front of a member of the human race. Again, if this is your first time, go get that banana speech we've been working on.

Practice once or twice by yourself after reviewing your three improvement areas as a refresher. Afterwards, find someone willing to listen to you. This can be a spouse, boyfriend, girlfriend, neighbor, stranger, friend, co-worker, etc. Who they are really doesn't matter as long as they are willing to provide honest feedback. If you are able (and want to add additional pressure), find a group of people to speak in front of.

After you get done speaking, ask what you could do to improve, and be ready to be open to any and all criticism. There really is no such thing as constructive or destructive criticism. There is only criticism. It is up to you to choose whether you will use it to your advantage in a constructive manner or let it destroy you. You, and only you, get to choose.

You: You really like ending thoughts with requiring me to choose between two options, don't you?

Yes. Yes, I do. Thanks for interrupting me. Now where was I? Oh yeah. Write down the feedback preferably in the same place you wrote down your own feedback from the day before.

If they are willing to listen to you again, give it another shot and try to apply the new feedback on the spot. If not, no worries! Thank them for their time and advice, and call it a day.

DAY 4

Day four is feedback review day. You should have a lot of feedback by now. Go back and review everything you wrote down so far. Today you're going to focus on making adjustments to yourself and your speech.

Looking over your feedback, do you notice patterns of behavior that show up multiple times? Does the same section of your speech never come out as clear as you want it? Do you consistently look down at the ground while you speak? Do you say filler words like "um" and "uh" between sentences? Make note of what feedback you keep getting the most and work on improving those. These areas will be the biggest bang for your buck as far as noticeable improvement goes.

When I first started watching my recordings for feedback, I noticed I mumbled like a mad man. I would cram eight words into one, and I had no idea I was doing it. In my head everything sounded crystal clear, but that was not the case in reality.

I knew that was an area, among others, that I could work on and notice an incredible amount of improvement. So I made extra effort to pronounce each and every word when I spoke. I noticed when I was tired, nervous, or just feeling lazy, I would mumble more often. I didn't realize just how much people would ask me to repeat what I was saying. I figured I was talking fast or their hearing sucked.

Come to find out that was not the case. Putting in the extra effort to pronounce my words resulted in drastic improvements. Do the same things with your feedback reviews, and you'll notice the same.

Work on what needs the most attention, but don't go overboard trying to make it perfect. It won't be.

As for your content, add anything you need to add for clarity, take out anything that is not essential, and rearrange and tighten up the organization with transitions if needed. Make it good enough, put a bow on it, make it your final draft, and call it a night.

If you want, take a moment and think back to the first time you spoke through your rough draft compared to today. Feel proud with the incredible work you've done so far and just how much you've improved.

DAY 5

Rehearse the final draft of your speech twice then find a quiet place, if you can, for the next exercise. You are going to visualize giving your speech to an audience. Olympian athletes and top performers do this all the time.

Several studies have even published research combining weight lifting and visualizing. Half of the group in these studies actually lifted weights for a period of time while the other half did NOT lift weights and just visualized lifting weights. The result? BOTH groups showed muscle growth and were able to lift more by the end of the study. That's incredible! That study showed the brain simply doesn't know the difference between reality and what we visualize. The bodily response was the same.

We'll use that trick to our advantage with public speaking. You ready?! Start by closing your eyes and visualize where you are going to be right before you speak. Your goal is to create a virtual reality of sorts by adding as much detail as you possibly can to the experience. The more details you have the better the results.

Do you know where you will speak? Visualize that place and where you might be right before you speak. If you don't know, simply imagine to the best of your ability. Is the speech indoors? Outdoors? Are you giving the speech in the morning? Late at night? What's the weather like? What are you wearing? A suit? Casual clothes? Are you on a stage? Standing at the far end of a conference table? What is your audience like? Children? Adults? How many people do you expect?

Bring all of these details into play to make it feel real to you. If you start to feel a little nervous (or really nervous) as if you are really about to speak in front of a crowd, then you are on the right track! This is the exact response we are looking for as it helps expand your tolerance for feeling uncomfortable, especially since your brain can't tell the different between visualizing and reality.

Imagine you are just about to speak, and you feel your nerves creep up on you, but you can keep them under control as you remember your nerves are just signaling this is important to you.

Picture yourself smiling and actually excited to speak. You know this is exactly where you need to be to grow as a speaker. You feel confident because you've practiced and practiced your speech more times than you can count.

Imagine you can hear, and even feel, the size of the crowd around you. You know they are just as human as you are and probably just as afraid to speak in front of a crowd. Maybe even more afraid than you are in that moment.

Now imagine you've just been called to speak, and you can feel your heart pounding harder, but you are not turning back. Your heart is ramping up, but you are in control. You breathe slowly and stand tall and confident as you make eye contact with the crowd.

Imagine taking one more deep breath while scanning the crowd in front of you (actually take a deep breath while visualizing). As soon as you can't consume another molecule of air, smile and exhale your first few words of your speech. Actually speak out loud while keeping your eyes closed and visualizing the crowd. Go through your entire speech from start to finish.

Once you are done with your speech, keep visualizing that moment. Notice the feeling you feel as you realize you faced your fears and you had nothing to be afraid of.

Open your eyes and take a moment to note how your feel. Is there a sense of relief? Is your heart beating a little faster? Did your body release a dose of adrenaline?

Simply take a mental note and get ready to do it again. Try and add in even more details this time, and make the audience even bigger! Double or triple the amount of people you're speaking in front of. Now go through the exercise again. Keep doing this for whatever time you have allotted yourself. When you are done, call it a day.

DAY 6

It's the day before you will speak. Today you want to bust through a few practice rounds of your speech. Shoot for three rounds, and then you are close to calling it a night. After practicing and writing down any additional feedback you want to capture, it's time to write down your game plan for Day 7: Speech Day.

Your game plan outlines what you will do that day, starting with the moment you wake up. Actually it starts the night before, but we'll get into that. Get out a piece of paper and something to write with.

To help you mentally see the amount of time you have to prepare, note when you speak and when you wake up.

You will also want to note where you will speak so you can plan for how much time you need to get there. As an example, I've filled in information as if you were going to give your banana speech to a Toastmasters club.

When: 5:30 pm

Where: Toastmasters club meeting at the local library

Wake up time: 7:00 am

In this example, you would have roughly 10.5 hours in between the moment your eyes open, and the moment you say the first word of your speech. Now ask yourself, "Does this give me enough time to squeeze in a handful of quick activities to prepare me for my speech along with everything else I had planned to get done that day?" If it does, great! Move on to the next section where we'll talk about said activities. If not, now is a good time to prioritize. Either wake up earlier (which is not always a great idea if you are not used to getting up earlier), or do what you can to make room for some prep work prior to your speech.

Speech day activities:

- Drink a large glass of water as soon as you wake up
- Recite your affirmation
- Exercise
- Do something that makes you feel alive
- Do something silly
- Journal your thoughts
- Practice your speech

These activities are my modified version of Hal Elrod's *Miracle Morning* activities (another great book I recommend). Do you have to do every single activity? No. These are just my recommendations. All of them help prepare you for your speech in their own unique way. I don't always do all of them. Sometimes I just don't have the time. You might even modify this to fit your particular style of prepping for a speech.

On your plan beneath where you wrote your wake-up time, write the activities you will do today as a to-do list.

CHAPTER 23

SPEECH DAY ACTIVITIES

DRINK WATER

As soon as you wake up drink some water (12 oz at least). That's a typical bottle of water.

While you sleep, you lose water that you need to replenish. Odds are you wake up dehydrated and don't even know it. Our bodies, especially our brains, need proper or adequate amounts of water to function at peak performance. Plus, that water will help flush out the grogginess from waking up.

Time: 2 Minutes

AFFIRMATION

Since you're not hunting for a job opportunity today, your affirmation changes.

"Today, I am a courageous speaker. I am prepared, confident and ready to give my speech. Even though I am prepared, I give myself permission to suck. I am confident I will grow from this experience, and I am absolutely ready to punch my fears. IN. THE. FACE!"

TIME: ~1 Minute

EXERCISE

Next you need to exercise, preferably outside. Being outside wakes up your senses from the sounds you hear, what you see, the feel from the change in temperature, and the smells you smell. With your senses waking up, exercise helps wake up the rest of your body: your heart, your lungs, your muscles, your blood system, etc.

The exercise is up to you and can be as easy as a brisk walk for 10 minutes or so. You don't have to crank it up to CrossFit insanity, and don't make it any more intense than what you are used to. Flipping tractor tires for the first time on the day of your speech is a recipe for disaster. The last thing you need is to overwork yourself or cause injury before you even have a chance to speak. Afterwards, you should feel much more awake and most likely feeling pretty good.

Take a shower afterwards if you need to. This is when I check off my activity that makes me feel alive.

Time: ~10 Minutes

DO SOMETHING THAT MAKES YOU FEEL ALIVE

I reward myself for exercising with a warm shower, but I end it with a freezing cold shower for about 30 seconds to a minute. The cold water shocks my body into existence. My heart races. My breathing is uncontrollable. Fight or flight kicks in, and I have to make a choice. Turn the shower back to warm, turn the shower off, or stick with it and fight it!

I choose to fight it, and soon fighting becomes embracing the cold shower. I can't help but send out a "WHOA!" as the water wakes up every cell in my body.

What feels like an eternity is really less than a minute in reality. Gradually, I start to control my breathing and my body starts to adapt. As I stop shaking, I think "This is actually okay. It doesn't matter if this continues or not because I'm going to be okay."

At that point, I end the shower. The water stops, and I feel amazing! Unstoppable even! I realized it's during those showers that I can't think of the past or the future. There is not a single worry, regret, or fear because I'm completely in the present.

You might find another way to feel alive whether that is listening to your favorite song, driving with the windows down to feel the wind, or stealing (seriously, don't do that last one). Whatever works and is readily available to fit into your day, do that!

I would highly recommend the cold shower because it's really hard to replicate that feeling, and it only takes less than a minute of your day. Secondly, just like with public speaking, you have to willingly choose to step into a place of discomfort (cold shower) while currently in a place of comfort (warm shower). You don't get that same effect listening to music or driving with the windows down because both of those situations don't create the mental barrier you must choose to break through.

Time: ~5 Minutes

Before we get into the other activities, do everything else that you usually do to start your day: get dressed for work, eat breakfast, get the kids ready for school, whatever. Get this stuff done so you're not thinking about what you need to do while doing the rest of your speech prep activities, which you can schedule at any time in the day.

REHEARSE YOUR SPEECH

Find some time in your day before you speak to rehearse your speech. If you can actually practice in the same place where you are expecting to speak, that's even better. Run through your speech a few times if you can, but know when to call it quits.

By now you've already practiced at least 15 times in the past week. Feel confident you've put in the necessary time and effort to properly prepare and feel assured you've put in more work than most speakers who might simply practice the night before or the morning of. Even if you still don't feel ready, remember that's just the old you talking. The new you has already given yourself permission to suck. You know by now sucking is the dues we pay to get better and grow.

Time: ~5–30 Minutes (depending on the length of your speech)

DO SOMETHING SILLY

Find some time to do something silly. This helps you to not take yourself so seriously, calms your nerves, and helps you to loosen up. Fear can strike a chord with our nerves that make us stiff and uptight. You need something to counteract that, and being silly, even borderline embarrassing, can do that. This can take a thousand different forms. If you think of doing something that makes you feel uncomfortable (yet legal) and causes you to smile, you should consider doing that. You are on the right track!

Below are a few things I've done. All of which my wife does not know about. Maybe she'll find out if she actually reads my book.

- Smiled at myself in a mirror for two minutes with the biggest, cheesiest grin on my face
- Went to McDonalds and ordered my food via singing. Lots of weird looks on this one.
- Danced in a Wal-Mart parking lot outside of my car while blaring a Taylor Swift song. I believe it was "Shake It Off."
- Went to a public bathroom (which I thought was empty) and practiced an evil laugh.

During that last one, someone in a stall asked in a really confused voice:

"Why are you doing that?"

His question scared the crap out of me (luckily, I was in a bathroom). I was already embarrassed, so I answered his question honestly.

"I have to give a speech, and I'm doing something silly to calm my nerves. . . ."

"Oh . . . that makes sense I guess. I get nervous too. Can I try?"

There was a bit of an awkward silence before I answered.

"Sure, why not."

At a certain point, it became a competition, and soon we started busting out laughing. The bathroom patron started stomping his feet from laughing, and I had to run to a urinal before I pissed in my pants. It turned out to be more than I needed to relax my nerves. I actually gave one of my better speeches that day. Thank you bathroom patron—whomever you are.

Spontaneous action is key here. If you think about it for too long, you'll most likely let the old you debate long enough to convince yourself not to.

Time: ~5 Minutes

—Cody's Note—

I've recently been experimenting with rejection therapy after reading *Rejection Proof* by Jia Jiang. I've been using rejection as my "do something silly" activity before I speak, and I'm seeing great results. I highly recommend reading his book to learn more about rejection therapy. Life changing.

JOURNAL YOUR THOUGHTS

I'll try and journal on a sheet of paper my thoughts about an hour before I go on stage, which is usually when I can feel my nerves get a little jumpy. I'll simply write down how I'm feeling and why, taking five minutes to write. I'll usually just write this down on my game plan paper. It's incredible how much clarity I can achieve in my mind by simply writing down how I feel and discovering why. If you do this, don't think about what you're going to write. Just write. It doesn't even have to be about how you're feeling.

Time ~5 Minutes

CONTROL YOUR NERVES

If at any point you start to feel your nerves get the better of yourself, plan to stop the fire before it spreads. What you choose to do can take many forms.

Whenever I feel my fear creeping up, I first recognize that I'm feeling nervous. This happens more frequently as the time between now and when I speak comes closer and closer. I'll take three deep, slow breathes as I visualize banishing my coward-self back to his cave. I'll then ask myself (and answer) out loud the following questions:

Why am I afraid?

—Well . . . because I'm afraid to look like an idiot and not be accepted in front of a lot of people.

Is that something I'm willing to accept in order to grow?

—Yes, I'm willing to accept that.

Is my audience full of people who are also afraid of speaking in front of people?

—Most likely.

Is my audience made up of perfect, flawless people who've never made mistakes?

—Definitely not!

Is my audience going to remember my performance and every mistake I make forever and ever?

—Nope. They are most likely going to forget everything five minutes after I finish speaking because they (just like me) are more consumed with what's going on with their own lives than someone else's.

I'll then take three more deep, slow breathes, and during my exhale, I'll wish my audience happiness. Wishing my audience happiness gets my mind off of myself and my nerves.

Lastly, I'll do something active like go for a brisk walk, do pushups, or squats. Something to keep me active, and I'll keep a huge grin on my face while I do it. That is my ritual, and I might do this a few times during the day, depending on how nervous I am. I'll even go through this ritual if I can right before I speak.

Time: ~10 Minutes

THAT'S IT!

That's the game plan in a nutshell. The only other thing I like to do before I speak is find someone (usually someone I know) who can either record me giving my speech or at least pay close attention to my performance and later give me feedback.

If I simply just ask someone afterwards how I did without giving them the task beforehand, I've noticed I hardly get any feedback at all. That made me realize just how little attention people pay or little they even notice any of my mistakes or flaws. This should come to you as a relief rather than a disappointment.

That's your full week at a glance. You'll be impressed how far you will improve from day one (mind mapping) versus your performance on the day you speak. Work pays off in the long run.

You: So do I have to do this every week from now on so I can control my fears?

Not necessarily. You'll start to really notice changes after 4–6 weeks of speaking once a week. After 3–4 months, you'll feel a greater sense of confidence and courage to really overcome your fears. At that point, you could easily go into maintenance mode by speaking twice a month.

I continue to speak at least once a week because I want to become a professional speaker, coach others, and eventually start speaking to bigger and bigger crowds to continue improving. I understand that for most people overcoming their fears is the ultimate goal, and they are completely comfortable stopping there.

CHAPTER 24

WHEN YOU DON'T HAVE A LOT OF TIME TO PREPARE

There will be times when you are given an opportunity to speak with zero time to prepare. Someone will ask you to speak with only a couple days, hours, or a few minutes to speak. It happens. Especially as you start speaking once a week, those around you will know you the go-to person for speaking engagements.

It's in these moments where it would be so easy to walk away declining the opportunities. But it's in those moments where we grow the most. When we don't feel prepared, yet we do it anyway.

Anyone can be courageous when they are fully prepared. It takes real courage to fight that internal instinct to run when you know there just isn't the time to become fully confident in your ability to perform.

Just remember when the opportunity arises for you to speak with little to no time to get ready, your coward-self will take the floor. She'll question you, doubt you, and be so kind as to put together a slide show displaying a persuasive and informative presentation on all the reasons why you should not go through with it and why you should buy a timeshare in Oklahoma instead.

Don't sign the contract and ignore your coward-self. She's all talk anyway. Say yes to the opportunity and realize just how far you've come.

So how do you prepare when there's little to no time? You go right back to the 7 principles of punching your fears in the face.

Give yourself permission to suck.

Running away from your fears actually makes things worse.

The only mistake is not trying.

It is okay to be nervous.

It is not about you.

Tell a story.

Know your audience is human.

You are really going to have to give yourself permission to suck. With little time to prepare, it's only natural to expect an uptick in the number of mistakes you make. Give yourself some grace knowing you will make mistakes. If you expect to make a few more than usual, you won't be surprised by them. It's also important to continue to remind yourself that it is more than okay to make mistakes because, otherwise, you would never learn anything, and you wouldn't grow.

When you say yes to a last-minute opportunity to speak, you've officially crossed off the second and third principles. You've done something that many people can't bring themselves to do. You've decided to face your fears and decided to at least try.

Remember that it's perfectly normal to feel nervous. That's just your body letting you know that you are taking this seriously. If you don't feel nervous in the slightest then you are probably not human. Even professional speakers still get a little nervous prior to speaking.

Knowing this speaking opportunity is not about you helps put everything into perspective. In the end, it's not about you or your fears. It's about serving your audience.

When you don't have a lot of time to prepare, tell a story if the situation permits itself. Having a story that goes along with your message will make it much easier to prepare rather than having to make up material. Tell a story you are already familiar with so you won't have to learn a whole bunch of new content in a short period of time. When you don't have a lot of time to prepare, stick with what you know.

Last but not least, know your audience is human. Know that they are not expecting you to be perfect, flawless, or a shining beacon of the pinnacle of human existence. Your audience will be made up of humans that can feel the fears and passions of others.

The greatest thing you can do on stage is show that you are human and vulnerable, yet courageous. Every single one of them has imperfections, insecurities, and hates eating kale just like you. Most importantly, humans forget.

Even if you completely bomb on stage, by morning most people in the audience, if not everyone, will have forgotten about you and any mistakes you made. The only one who will truly remember your performance will be you and you alone.

And with that, my journey with you has come to an end. It is now my pleasure to turn you back over to Shasta who is going to go over some quick, not so obvious teachers' tips that I'm sure you will enjoy.

Teachers, thank you for what you do. I had several teachers growing up that had a huge impact on my life, and I can only imagine the many lives you influence on a daily basis.

You've got some fear punching to do, so go out there and become a courageous speaker, a courageous teacher, and your most courageous-self.

Welcome to the Stage Fight Club.

SECTION 5

—

ADVICE FROM THE FIELD

CHAPTER 25

GOLD STARS FROM THE LONE STAR

I am a small-town farm girl from Texas, and if you don't believe me, just listen to me talk. To all you non-Texans, there are four things that all Texans have in common: our love of Jesus, football, John Wayne, and the Lone Star State.

In Texas we have a phrase *tienes ganas* which literally means to have want or desire. To be a farmer in Texas, you have to want it. You have to make sacrifices. You have to be bold. You have to take risks. You have to earn it through blood, sweat, and tears. And once you've earned it, only then will you see the beauty that comes from Texas Red Dirt.

My first year teaching in Texas, I taught kindergarten. I know the ideas we all have of teaching kindergarten: snacks, nap time, arts and crafts, red rover, ect. But let me tell you something about kindergarten teachers, they have a special place reserved for them in heaven. Teaching kindergarten is like juggling swords that are on fire while riding on a unicycle and singing your ABCs backwards! Kidding, kind of.

I earned every gold star that I have on my teaching chart during my time in kindergarten! Kindergarten taught me valuable lessons: Always bring an extra set of clothes because at some point during the year, you will be covered in someone else's vomit! The rules of the English language make no sense to a five year old trying to sound out the word “light”. Cheerios in the toilet are a must if you wish for little boys to aim correctly.

And nothing can prepare you for graduation day. Bring extra tissues, YOU WILL NEED THEM MORE THAN THE PARENTS!

It comes as no surprise to me that educators everywhere have chosen Red as the color of our educational movement. Because if we are ever truly going to stand in professional solidarity, we must become bold. We must sacrifice. We must have *ganas*. And, when all of the red dust settles, only then will the rest of the world see the beauty of a teacher.

—Shasta’s Note—

Always carry a Tide stain remover pen. It’s the bomb.edu at removing all kind of kinder stains, even throw up!

CHAPTER 26

GRIT, THE BREAKFAST OF CHAMPIONS

Four years into my teaching career, I fell in love with a handsome, blue-eyed Mississippi Airman who would take me far away from my beloved Texas.

Moving twenty-two hours away and leaving my top-performing school was hard. Leaving my hometown (population 431 if you count the cows) was even harder—especially after learning the starting salary for South Carolina teachers.

But, despite every challenge, my desire to learn and grow from the people of South Carolina remained.

During my time there, I quickly saw the grit of all South Carolinians as the state rallied together through floods, hurricanes, and the Emanuel African Methodist Episcopal Church tragedy. Through every challenge, with the world watching, South Carolina stood strong and resilient.

Therefore, my message to you fellow teachers is to embody the spirit of "Carolina Grit" in a profession that on average has a 70% turnover rate within the first five years. Because right now, more than ever, our profession needs resiliency. I want you to teach your students to be resilient in a time when our nation's schools are marred with devastation. And once more, with the world watching, I am asking teachers in my own district in South Carolina to stand for more than ourselves. I am asking educators everywhere to stand up for communities, for public education, and for our kids. Texas may have taught me how to want something, but South Carolina has taught me how to stand for something.

For this reason, no matter where I go or what I do, I will forever carry with me the lessons that I've learned here in this great state, ones of resiliency and strength. Each of my colleagues have instilled in me the true grit of South Carolina, and for that, I am truly grateful.

—Shasta's Note—

In the South, grits are an actual breakfast food! I prefer mine smothered in cheese.

CHAPTER 27

AND THE WINNER IS. . .

During my time in South Carolina, I also had the honor of being named District Teacher of the Year. Now, although it is an incredible honor, I want all you non-teachers to know when you win a prestigious title such as this in education, You get—drum roll please—ABSOLUTELY NOTHING!

Not a bonus, not a stipend. ZIP. ZERO. ZILCH (unless you have an awesome district like mine, thank you Sumter).

But, for the first time, you have a platform, and other professionals in your community want to hear what you have to say. They all want to know teaching tips and secrets of the trade. So, in this chapter, I have decided to share with you my opinion of what makes an outstanding teacher.

I suspect my futile effort to create a definitive list is doomed to fail because outstanding teachers are as diverse as the students they teach. As a student, I would have said a great teacher was entertaining and gave very little homework. But now, I would say outstanding teachers are only the reflection of the outstanding teachers before them.

I fondly remember my Spanish teacher's fervor as she spoke about *El Dia de Los Muertos*. We all laughed as she taught us the Spanish mantra of hope to the tune of the Fresh Prince, but to this day, I can still proudly recite in perfect Spanish: *Con esperanza, nada es imposible.*

Now, each time that I "Hit the Quan" or "Whip and Nae Nae" to motivate my students to master their multiplication facts, I understand that a teacher's passion has no bounds. A teacher's passion can manifest itself within anyone and change their entire perception of themselves as a learner. True passion is meant to be shared, and each day that I get to share my love of learning is a good day.

While teaching is a gift that comes naturally to some, outstanding teachers work tirelessly to create a challenging, nurturing, positive environment for learning. I have found that teaching will demand all that you can give, and then some. Yet, good teachers always have enough sense of self to survive those days.

My earliest memories of school are of my kindergarten teacher, Mrs. K. We didn't get off to the best start. I cried for my mom the entire first month, and each morning she pried my tiny fingers from my mother's leg. She would wipe my tears and begin my day with a gentle hug. She spoke softly, and her composure never wavered no matter how loud I screamed. So, each day I remember to give gentle hugs and cool high fives, to speak when words are needed, and to share the silence when they are not. Most importantly, when days are challenging, I remember to be my students' own Mrs. K.

To be a reflection of someone, you must in turn be reflective. Teaching requires a willingness to cast a critical eye on your practice, pedagogy, and self. Sometimes that process can be brutal. An outstanding teacher will always be a lifelong learner and embrace constructive efforts to improve their teaching. Each day, I try to have enough humility to realize that teaching is not about my ego. Equally as important in reflecting about what went well or did not go well is the understanding that often things go right because of what the students bring to the lesson.

I believe that every child needs a champion—someone in their corner to fight for them, to cheer them on, and to lift them up.

My high school basketball coach, Coach K, was my champion in life when I needed one dearly. He was the only teacher waiting for me with arms open wide the day that I buried my beloved best friend.

And, at my high school graduation ceremony, he was there cheering loudly as I crossed the stage. For as long as I live, I will never forget his compassionate gesture. Because I know the true worth of a champion, I strive to be a champion for my students every day. I wipe their tears, cheer them on, visit hospital rooms. Tragically, at times, I even tuck a favorite Dr. Seuss book into a tiny kindergartener's casket as a final act of love.

You see, these moments are ones that they do not teach you in class. But, these moments are what make you a champion. Being your students' champion when they need you the most is what makes you an outstanding teacher.

I am an outstanding teacher only because I have had outstanding teachers to emulate. Each day I try to be the teacher that I would want my child to have. I try to reflect the qualities of all those before me that fostered my love for learning. Each day I pay homage to their tireless efforts and investment into my life, and hopefully, I too am my students' champion.

CHAPTER 28

FORTUNE COOKIE

I am addicted to Chinese food! I would eat chicken fried rice for every meal if my husband would allow it. But, my favorite part actually comes at the end, reading my fortune from the cookie.

After being named a finalist teacher for my district, my husband took me out for Chinese to celebrate. But, at the end of the meal, there was no fortune inside of my cookie.

Devastated, I immediately took this as a bad omen. However, my waitress informed me that when you receive a cookie with no fortune, it is an opportunity to write your own.

Even though there is no Chinese legend or proverb to prove her cookie wisdom true, I have always loved her sentiment. My biggest piece of advice to you is to write your own fortune when it comes to teaching. If I could gift you with some fortune cookie wisdom it would be:

Lead that professional development

I know, I know, in teacher world, professional development days are like staff meetings that NEVER END. But truthfully, professional development is a time for teachers to seek out new learning to better improve student achievement. Leading a professional development gives you a platform to share your ideas with other professionals. It affords you the opportunity to stretch yourself professionally, share what you are passionate about, and directly influence the instruction of fellow teachers. So, next time you get the dreaded professional development email, sign-up to lead the session. You just might surprise yourself with how much you enjoy it!

Advocate

Advocate is probably one of the most terrifying verbs for educators. We hear it constantly. "Teachers, please advocate for...."

But, most teachers are still trying to discover their own teacher voice and learn what true advocacy is.

Once you figure out the issues that matter to you:

remember to only speak for yourself

do your research

know why this issue matters

know who has the means to change this particular issue

and most importantly, know that you are the only person who can give your students a voice

Advocacy is a large vision; therefore, start small. Advocate within your school, your district, your community, and then in your state and nation. Some easy ways to advocate are to write letters, invite community members into your classrooms, vote in local and state elections, join your local teaching forum, and get involved with teacher organizations in your state. The only goal you should have in advocacy is to establish teaching as a respected and influential profession. Because until teachers are respected and viewed as professionals, our needs and the needs of our students will never be met.

Always take Mental Health Days throughout the year

As educators, taking a day off is often more trouble than it's worth. Sub plans are the worst, you worry about your kids all day, and then you mentally prepare yourself for the mess that will be your classroom the following day.

My first experience with a sub was a bit traumatic for this OCD control freak.

I was teaching kindergarten at the time, so I paid due diligence to detail, outlining the day basically down to the minute because, remember, I am a perfectionist. I wanted the substitute to leave saying that my class was wonderful!

However, all my organizational efforts were in vain. I walked into my room the next day to find RED FINGER PAINT ALL OVER MY CENTER TABLE, books everywhere, and nothing in its ordinary place! How five-year-olds manage to get my red finger paint out of a locked cabinet remains a mystery to me.

Despite all the sub horror stories, we still need mental health days. Teaching is exhausting, and if we don't take care of ourselves, we cannot take care of our students. So my suggestion to you is to take at least one mental health day a semester, and on this day: Netflix and chill, turn off your Remind app or Class Dojo, don't check your work email, go to the bathroom whenever you want, and enjoy the quiet!

Seek out your teaching person(s)

The teaching world is full of challenges: fidget spinners, homemade slime, the Floss, and songs about baby sharks that test the limits of your patience. In all of this, it's good to know that someone's got your back or at least a hidden stash of chocolate for those really bad days.

In the teaching world, everyone has to find their "teaching person". This is the one person who will share expo markers with you, knows exactly what you are thinking at a faculty meeting by the look on your face, will geek out over educational Mr. Miyagi's with you, and can talk you off of a ledge when you have taught for four straight weeks and your students still can't find a common denominator.

This is the person who helps you when your mom has emergency surgery by emailing the principal, copying your lesson plans, making sure your kids behave for the substitute, and showing up at the hospital with sweet tea and Chick-fil-A.

Once you're lucky enough to find such a teaching person, hold on to them, appreciate them, and know teaching life is much better with them in it!

Treat every person with respect, especially those hard-to-handle parents

Teachers everywhere have their own parent horror story. We see all types: the helicopter parent, the parent who thinks their child is perfect, the parent who never shows, the parent who is on their phone the entire meeting, the parent who knows what's best for their child despite your years of professional training, and the prosecutor parent.

But the truth is: Parents are our partners. They are their child's first educator, and they ALWAYS deserve our respect. After the first day of school, I personally call EVERY SINGLE parent to introduce myself, to learn about their child, and to start the year off on a positive note.

But before I call them, I look them up on Facebook or Instagram. I'll admit; it's a little stalkerish, but after that day, I will be responsible for their entire world, so I owe it to them to take a peek inside their life. I see them smiling with their kids in Halloween costumes, baking Christmas cookies, their summer vacation pictures from the beach, them standing over their little princess as she blows out her birthday candles, cheering at their son's soccer game, and I notice that they too dislike Alabama football.

I read their posts about long days at the office, small victories in potty training, and missing their kids while they are deployed.

I check their Facebook and Instagram because it reminds me that most parents are truly trying their best. It quiets the rage in my heart when Susie shows up with no coat in the winter or when little Bobby's parents didn't show up for the play even after he won the lead role.

It reminds me that every person deserves respect. Because when I am up late trying to figure out how to make my students understand multiplying fractions, I am not alone.

Their parents are up late sewing a Superman cape, writing little notes in lunch boxes, wondering if they are doing this whole parent thing right, and possibly even watching YouTube videos to relearn how to multiply fractions because apparently we teachers changed math.

Invest in the whole child

When I started my career, I loved kids, but my main focus was on student achievement. As a teacher, I am evaluated on how well my students progress academically and score on standardized state tests. I wanted all of my sweet kinder babies reading on E's before they left me and structuring numbers to ten like young mathematicians. I worked very hard at perfecting my craft until a cold October morning when my teaching life was changed forever.

There was a fire. Two of my former students were involved. They were cousins, but honestly, they were more like brothers.

We had just had fire safety week at school. So I analyzed my every action that week. Did I truly make sure they understood what to do in a fire emergency? Did they know to trust the fireman?

I cried out for God to protect my sweet kinder babies. Later the next morning, I learned one of my students was now fatherless, but alive. Tears streamed down my face as I searched for the paper that he had wrote titled "My Dad is my Hero!"

I held out hope that his cousin was also alive, but he was not as fortunate.

Although he wasn't in my homeroom class, he was a part of my afternoon reading and math group, and I began to replay every memory I had of him.

I could see his mischievous grin, I could feel his tiny hand in mine.

I could hear him say, "Mrs. Gibson, watch me climb to the very top!"

He was fearless. He was bold. And, no logic existed to explain why he would never have any other graduations except kindergarten.

I wept that night for all the life breathed into him by his family, teachers and loved ones: The juice boxes, the peanut butter and jelly sandwiches with the crust cut off, the bedtime stories, the hugs, the I love yous, and all the life that he would never lead.

At the funeral, all I kept thinking was: I never got to see him play football. He begged me to come watch him play, and I never did.

On that day, it didn't matter what reading level he was on, and every day since then, it hasn't mattered to me either. Teaching is about more than test scores and job evaluations. Teaching is about small moments of grace, laughter, and experiences. Teaching is about the whole child.

Now I make it a point to invest in my students' lives outside of the classroom. I give secret handshakes, play GAGA ball at recess every chance I get, eat lunch weekly with my kiddos, and give BIG graduation hugs!

My sweet kinder baby would be in fifth grade, the grade I now teach.

Some days I look at my students and wonder if he would look similar. Would he be that tall? Would he still like math more than reading? Would he still live life fearlessly? And, on sunny days, while I watch my students play football, I whisper to him words of regret and gratitude.

Be prepared for teaching to break your heart

If you are looking for the cookie-cutter teaching advice book, this is not it.

I truly love my job and my students, but this is about TEACHING in REAL LIFE. There is a reason that we have such a teacher shortage in America. But no one likes to talk about what lies beneath the surface because if we truly unmasked the horror, we would be left with only our own marred image. For years, we have either villainized teachers or placed them on martyred pedestals. I have been disrespected, hit, kicked, and spat on by children. I loved them anyway.

I have had parents tell me that I am worthless, that I am the worst teacher they have ever encountered, and I should seriously consider a new profession. I loved their children anyway.

I have gone years without a raise, had horrible insurance, worked part-time jobs, and bought school supplies with my own money. I loved teaching anyway.

But I can no longer sugar coat the realities of the teaching profession. Teaching in real life is having your heart broken every single day.

I once loved a student so fiercely, I asked my fiancé if we could adopt him. He was one of eight children. Both of his parents were struggling with addiction. He was born with fetal alcohol syndrome, and I wanted so badly to love him all the rest of his days.

I remember when I held him as I told him that I could not be his mommy.

I wiped his tears, and I whispered in his ear, "One day, your mommy will choose you, baby."

I left a piece of my shattered heart with him. We all have our demons, and regardless of my heartbreak, I have no right to judge his birth mother.

To this day, I still pray for the faceless, nameless woman to choose her son over addiction. People hear stories like this and want to put me on a pedestal and call me a saint, but I never wanted any of their praise or labels. I only wanted to be called mom.

There are thousands of other teachers out there with stories similar to mine. And then there are the martyrs, like young Victoria Soto, Colleen Ritzer, and Scott Beigl who gave their life for the teaching profession they loved. This is the reality of teaching in America. And right now, all I am is mad about that reality. Mad about what it does to me, what it did to them, and what it will do to every person who chooses the teaching life.

—Shasta's Note—

Math has not changed!

Gaga Ball is basically dodgeball on steroids in a wooden cage-like octagon. And yes, I do feel like Russell Crowe in Gladiator every time I step inside that arena!

Thank you: Anja, Jamie, Meredith, Rachel, Rebecca, and Rhonda for being my teaching person throughout my career.

Ron Antinori and Matt Miller, if you are reading this, I heart you. Thank you both for being my teaching Mr. Miyagi.

Check out Matt Miller's blog: Ditch that Textbook. It will change your life!

CHAPTER 29

STANDING OVATION

Amidst the heartbreak, anger, teacher shortage, educational policies, school safety, and high stakes testing, we must never forget that we are very fortunate to work in the field of education. There is no other profession quite like ours. We get to dress up like our favorite Dr. Seuss character. We get to immerse ourselves in the latest pop culture. We get to have secret handshakes. We get to be there for first dances and prom pictures, college acceptance letters, and life achievements.

We have reached the end of the lesson. But before you get your gold star, it's time for you to write your own teaching fortune. To speak out. To be resilient. To be courageous. To have *ganas* and grit. To punch your teaching fears in the face!

Most of all remember, you are incredible. You matter. You are capable of more than you can imagine. You are a TEACHER. You are a DIFFERENCE MAKER. And when you feel alone or like a failure, look for your stage fight brothers and sisters. We are the ones #wearingRedforED, giving you a standing ovation. I believe R.J. Palacio sums it up quite nicely in her quote:

"I think there should be a rule that everyone in the world should get a standing ovation at least once in their lives."

—Shasta's Note—

Thank you for letting me finally end with a quote. If you haven't read the book *Wonder*, it will change your life.

EVERYONE GETS A GOLD STAR!!!!

REQUEST FOR REVIEWS

What did you think about *Stage Fight for Teachers*?

First and foremost, thank you purchasing *Stage Fight for Teachers* and making it literally to the end of this book. Out of all the books at your disposal you chose this one and we are forever thankful. You invested your time and energy into getting this far, and I hope, beyond a shadow of a doubt, it was time and energy well spent.

If you enjoyed the book, can you do us a fist-bump solid? Please submit a review of *Stage Fight for Teachers* on Amazon. This allows other to-be courageous speakers more easily find this book, and also helps me refine and hone my writing to improve this and all future writing projects to come.

As always, you can reach Cody at:

Cody@stagefightclub.com

All the best to you and your journey,

Cody and Shasta

ABOUT THE AUTHORS

Cody Smith is passionate about the power of public speaking, and even more passionate about teaching & coaching others to punch their own fears in the face. Cody's mission is to give people actionable steps to quickly become courageous speakers.

When he's not speaking, coaching, or writing he loves:

- Eating cheesecake
- Throwing boomerangs
- Trying to catch boomerangs
- Playing with his 2 year old (which is like playing with a smaller, smarter version of himself)
- Hosting fake job interviews with random strangers inside elevators
- Not speaking in third person about himself

Cody is currently crushing several new writing projects waiting to be published.

You can connect with Cody via email:

Cody@stagefightclub.com

Shasta Smith is the 2018/2019 Sumter School District Teacher of the Year. She has 7 years of teaching experience.

She has used public speaking to build a platform from which to speak on. She has presented at the Oklahoma Reading Association, the Midwestern State University TAIR Bilingual Conference, and The Sumter E3 Conference where she has spoken in front of anywhere from 50 to 500 hundred people.

When she's not teaching or speaking, She's:

- Trying to beat her husband at Ping Pong. She beat him once and has not played him since.
- Eating tacos
- Running. . . So she can eat tacos with sour cream. Mmhmm, sour cream.
- Working on a line of children's books

ACKNOWLEDGEMENTS

To my co-writer, Shasta. Thanks for going on this adventure with me. You have been an absolute treasure to work with. The experiences you shared made me laugh, cry, and appreciate the impact teachers have had on my life.

OTHER BOOKS BY CODY

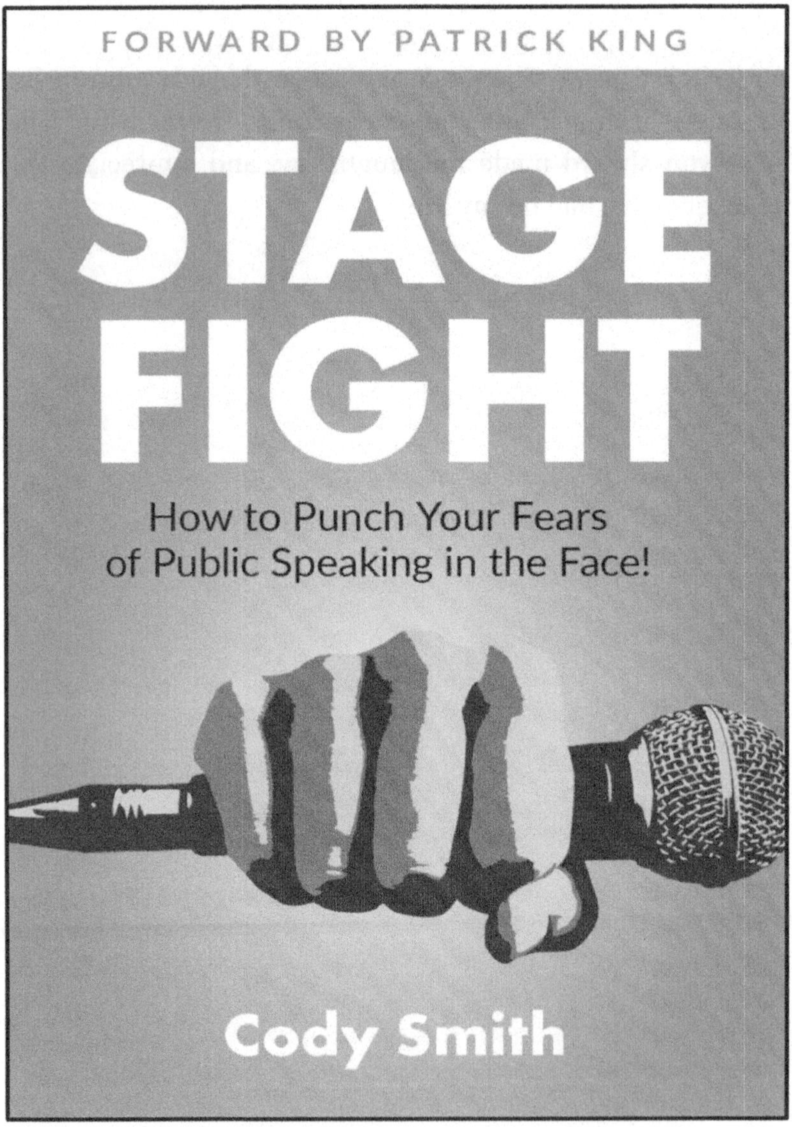

KICK
START
HOW TO SUCCESSFULLY FUND YOUR FIRST CROWDFUNDING CAMPAIGN ON KICKSTARTER.
CODY SMITH

COURAGEOUS SPEAKER COACHING PROGRAM WITH CODY SMITH

There are a thousand and one ways to get from A to B. Some are faster than others. With speed comes saving life's most limited resource: Time—which waits for no one.

Sprinting from A to B without a map or on a familiar route can lead to getting nowhere fast unless you have the support and guidance from someone whose has already trail blazed that path who can show you the ropes.

Put fuel to the fire on your journey to become a courageous speaker by hiring a coach and mentor. Hiring me as a coach will put you on the path of the straight and narrow as we collaborate together to identify your fears, address your key areas to see the most improvement in the fastest amount of time, and add a critical dose of accountability and mentorship to bring your public speaking to the next level and beyond.

If you decide to work with me and commit to conquering your fears of public speaking, you will:

- Pinpoint limiting beliefs, negative affirmations, and thought patterns that are preventing you from reaching your goals
- Develop a custom-tailored plan to face your fears public speaking on a weekly basis

- Get advice and guidance from someone who has truly walked a mile (or two) in your shoes
- Receive priceless feedback on your speeches each and every week to super charge your speaking improvement
- Get the accountability you need to stick to your custom plan
- Build lasting confidence to speak in front of an audience even when you are afraid
- Learn tried and true strategies to punch your fears in the face!

If you are serious about becoming a courageous speaker, then contact me at Cody@stagefightclub.com and we'll see if you are a good fit for the Courageous Speaker Coaching Program.

SPEAKER REQUEST

Could your group, organization, or corporation benefit by going beyond the content of this book to dominate the fear of public speaking to vastly improve the confidence and communication of your team?

Are you interested in contacting Cody for:

- A Stage Fight workshop for your workplace full of public speaking fear punching and courage building to boot
- Speaking engagements on conquering the fear of public speaking

To invite Cody to speak at your next event, get in touch with him directly through his website's contact form at

Cody@stagefightclub.com